WHAT PARENTS AND EDUCATORS SAY ABOUT THIS BOOK

"This book really changed my life. It's been two years and many of the lessons
I learned are still with me."
Sandra Pimetel, mother of three

"The focus of the book was right on. As a parent I think I was focused a lot more on my
childs' behavior than on my own. This class allowed me to refocus my attention on
myself and see how important that is with regard to my relationship with my daughter."
Victor Goode, father of one

"I now instill in my children that whatever they do in life is their own choice."
Nicole Brandford –Cambell, mother of three

"I learned that it was better to share than hold things inside."
Christine Boston, grandmother of four

"I choose peace over war and use all the techniques to establish this peace. Since I began
using Masterful Parenting techniques with my family, the atmosphere in my home has
become much more peaceful."
Roberto de la Rosa, parent of three

"The words Create, Promote, Allow, is something everyone already knows, but we just
don't recognize it in our life. Once we take control, once we feel we are responsible for
everything that happens, then we have a part in it. If we face that first as opposed to
blaming, we will succeed. This is very powerful."
Mark Etienne, teacher, New York Family Acadamy

"What I got out of this book was the ability to stop and look at a situation prior to reacting. Now I really think about what I want as the outcome and then decide to act."
Bruce Milner, father of one, Onteora High School

"In life we really need someone to show us the way. This book was my guide."
Nancy Pereita, mother of one

"Many of the hundreds of parents who have participated in your programs have shared
that it has helped them with their child's school life as well as with their family life. They
are better able to communicate with their children as well as their spouse."
Jorge Izquerdo, Superintendent District 6, NYC (representing 31,000 children)

You have seen the flower
As it blooms;
It takes a whole week
Before it opens.
If you pry it open
With your nails,
You loose the scent

—Akhter Ahsen, *Manhunt in the Desert*

MASTERFUL PARENTING

THE BOOK YOU WISH YOUR PARENTS HAD READ

DR. MARC ROSENBAUM

Copyright © 2004
Ariel Press
PO Box 674
Mt. Marion, New York 12456
www.ed4excellence.com

ISBN: 0-9753540-2-7

MASTERFUL PARENTING

CONTENTS

INTRODUCTION   7

1   CHOICE   15

2   WHO'S REALLY LISTENING?   27

3   TAKE CARE OF YOURSELF SO YOU CAN
HELP TAKE CARE OF OTHERS   45

4   REFLECTION BEFORE ACTION –
HOW YOU RELATE TO THE ISSUE IS THE ISSUE   53

5   ACCEPTANCE   61

6   RESPONSIBILITY – WHO'S CONTROLLING YOUR LIFE?   73

7   FORGIVENESS   81

8   COMMUNICATION – IT AIN'T WHAT YOU SAY...OR IS IT?   91

9   EMOTIONAL UNDERSTANDING   107

10   PRACTICING POSITIVE DISCIPLINE THROUGH THE
UNDERSTANDING OF YOUR CHILD'S TEMPERAMENT   117

11   RESOLVING CONFLICT PEACEFULLY   141

12   IRRATIONAL BELIEFS AND DESTRUCTIVE HABITS   153

13   TRUST AND CONTROL   175

ACKNOWLEDGMENTS

I am eternally grateful to four of my mentors: Seymour Fliegel, Dr. Harvey Kaye, Jamal Young and Dr. Anthony Palomeni. They saw value in my work and gave me the opportunity to present my programs before it was popular to do so.

Thanks to Cheryl Lugo and my dear friends Heide Banks and Howard Lazar for their valuable advice and ongoing support. I would also like to thank the teachers who gave me the knowledge and spiritual insight that made it possible for me to grow and eventually share what I have learned. Thanks to Fritz Perls, Oscar Ichazo and Swami Muktananda who, at the beginning of my search, awakened me to experiencing that I was more than my mind, body and emotions. A special thank you to Melba Alhonte who has become a cherished friend as well as an invaluable collaborator. Thanks also to Drs. Ron and Mary Hulnick, the presidents of the University of Santa Monica, and to John-Roger who taught me and continues to teach me how to practically apply my earlier wisdom in the world while becoming a more loving and compassionate human being.

PROLOGUE

I have found that the best way to teach children to learn and assimilate the knowledge, skills and behavior that will allow them to be successful in the world is to educate and transform the people who have the greatest influence on their lives: their parents. The first step in this transformation is to change from being obsessed with our children's behavior to becoming aware of and responsible for our own behavior.

In 1992, I left a highly successful twenty-year career as a dental surgeon to pursue my vision of teaching children personal transformation. This vision had its inception in a childhood where I was taught very little about the consequences of my choices or how to effectively deal with others' needs. Until learning and practicing specific social and emotional principles, I was often in trouble and engaged in disruptive and unfulfilling relationships.

Thirty years ago, in an effort to deal with my problems, I began to explore the teachings of various spiritual traditions and to study with several leading practitioners in the human potential movement. This gave me the impetus to pursue a Master's of Education in Theology and to earn a Master's in Applied Psychology. Slowly but surely, over many years, I've learned how to be truly happy and function as a more effective, conscious and loving human being.

The journey of self-exploration was the most important choice I ever made. If only I had learned as a child how to take responsibility for my life and to recognize, understand and effectively deal with my emotions – instead of always blaming others for my suffering – my early years might have been far less painful and far more productive. This life-changing exploration motivated me to create the Self-Mastery program, based on the premise that in order to be an effective teacher, parent or student, we must first be an effective human being.

During eleven years of presenting the Self-Mastery program to more than 3000 students, parents and teachers, I have found that the quality of the participants' lives improves as they explore options such as taking responsibility rather than blaming others, forgiving instead of harboring feelings of hatred or resentment, assertively communicating rather than being habitually passive or aggressive, and having empathy and acceptance rather than judging themselves and others.

Masterful Parenting is not about teaching the latest "techniques" that are guaranteed to bring parental bliss. This is a practical manual designed to educate, motivate and lead you through a series of precise exercises that will show you how your attitudes, beliefs and behavior affect your children. **By becoming more aware in each moment, you will find your own unique way of managing your life as well as contributing to the lives of your children.** As you learn how to truly serve yourself, you will become a guiding light for your children and become the best parent you can possibly be.

You can learn a great deal by just reading this book. But along with your reading, if you also complete the exercises, I promise you a new world of personal transformation and family satisfaction.

INTRODUCTION

MASTERFUL PARENTING:
THE BOOK YOU WISH YOUR PARENTS HAD READ

In order for change to be significant, parenting must be approached at the level of an individual transformation that requires courage and commitment.

The fact that you are reading this book is an indication that you are a parent who deeply cares about your children's well being. You are not alone. In my teaching experience, I've yet to meet a parent who didn't want a fulfilling relationship with their children and desire that their children excel in every aspect of life. But somewhere between the time a child takes their first step and when they walk down the aisle to receive a diploma, we realize that parenting is not as easy as we thought it would be.

7

As parents trying our best to raise children, we often find ourselves frustrated by their apathy, troublesome behavior, destructive habits and inconsistent academic performance. In many cases, conflict and alienation have replaced our vision of a relationship based on mutual caring, cooperation, trust and respect. This disharmony in our homes is being mirrored in society by escalating crime, pregnancy, suicide and, drug and alcohol abuse rates among our youth. As parents we search for answers.

WHAT IS THE SOLUTION?

It's easy to blame a government we believe to be unjust, other parents whom we judge as not caring enough, and today's children for their alleged apathy. However, there is a more responsible explanation for the discord in our families and society – one that provides us not only with hope but also with the tools to reverse the trend.

The answer lies in education, a type of education that develops the intelligence that has been shown to improve our health, relationships, academic performance and the achievement of our goals. **It is the intelligence that gives us the ability to observe and reflect on the relationship we have with ourselves, others and the world around us before taking action. When developed, this intelligence leads us to make choices that better serve ourselves and others and prepares us to deal with life and its challenges more effectively.**

This intelligence goes beyond the ability to memorize facts. We have spent years of education focusing on math, science, reading, writing – even dancing, drawing and athletics. But in order for our children to become truly knowledgeable, responsible and caring human beings, we must teach this social and emotional learning with the same structure and attention that has been devoted to traditional subjects.

8

WE CANNOT GIVE WHAT WE NEVER GOT

In an ideal world this necessary social and emotional learning would be an integral part of our children's schooling. But most schools do not have the resources, time or qualified instructors to effectively teach this type of intelligence. In most instances, the only place a child can receive this type of education is in the home.

After several years of presenting the Self-Mastery program to students, I observed that many of them would demonstrate valued principles in their lives only to have them not supported at home. As a result, they often returned to prior negative habits. But we cannot teach what we do not know. Some of us were fortunate enough to have emotionally intelligent parents as role models, but most of us were not. How are we supposed to demonstrate compassion, forgiveness, acceptance, communication and listening skills if we were never taught how to incorporate these qualities into our lives? It's as ludicrous as asking students to solve a complicated math problem without ever teaching them basic arithmetic.

We have consistently found that the best way to foster social-emotional learning for our children is to educate the people who have the greatest influence on their lives: their parents. For this reason, approximately 80 percent of the Self-Mastery courses are now being presented to parents.

ALL YOU NEED IS LOVE

In a study published in the *Journal of the American Medical Association* in 1997, researcher Michael Resnick at the University of Minnesota reported that teenagers who felt loved and connected to their parents had a significantly lower incidence of teenage pregnancy, substance abuse, violence and suicide. This parent-child bonding is created by spending quality time with a child where listening, loving, physical contact (e.g., caressing, kissing and making eye contact) and doing things that your child enjoys take place. These findings are not surprising...but why is it so difficult for many of us to achieve this level of connectedness with our children?

Love and connectedness are difficult to manifest when dealing with life outside our homes. But ironically, they can be just as hard to demonstrate when relating to the people we love the most: our family. This seems like a paradox – shouldn't it be easier to be loving with those who are the closest to us? My observation has been the opposite: the people we love are the ones who most often challenge our emotional stability. **Anger is not the opposite of love but is a response to the hurt we feel because we love.** If we observe the pattern, we will see that anger is a response to specific hurts that only those close to us can elicit – such as feeling abandoned, disrespected, taken advantage of, not being heard or betrayed. Our loved ones challenge our emotional stability and ability to "do the right thing" just because we love them. It's not only the way it is, it's the way it's supposed to be. **It has been said that the function of love is to bring up everything that is not loving.** This is done to heal the residual hurt that is left over from when we were children. Because we are so much more emotionally vulnerable, we need a lot of internal support to manifest the intelligence necessary when dealing with family challenges. The understanding and embodiment of principles brought forward in this book will enhance the development of this necessary internal support.

THE ESSENTIAL TOOL IS AWARENESS

The foundation of social-emotional intelligence is the ability to be aware of our thoughts, actions and feelings as they occur. By looking at ourselves in the present moment without judgment, we see how our attitudes and behavior affect us and everyone else in our lives. As we develop the ability to be aware, we discover patterns in our responses to certain situations. These patterns or habitual reactions are automatic, predictable and almost always inappropriate. They are the primary source of the pain that we cause ourselves and others.

For example, a parent participant shared a story about the time she was waiting with her husband and their five children for their plane to depart. The flight was canceled and rescheduled to a nearby airport. Upon their arrival at the other airport, that plane was canceled. She spoke about how she would usually get upset and find someone to yell at. This time, after taking a moment to be aware of her habitual response, she was able to remain calm by consciously reflecting on the futility of being upset in this situation.

Through awareness, we discover that we have more choices than we realize. We come to see, perhaps for the first time, what is best for ourselves and before long we develop the ability to see what really is best for our children as well as others in our lives. **Awareness makes it possible to respond to life and its challenges with openness and compassion**

THE 13 PRINCIPLES OF SELF-MASTERY

With awareness as the foundation, there are 13 principles of self-mastery to embody on the path to becoming masterful parents. Embodying these principles is a two-fold process: First, we must learn them and second, we must adopt them as the basis of our relationship with our children.

When we integrate these principles into our daily lives, everyone benefits. The 13 principles of self-mastery are:

1.   There is Always a Choice

2.   Listen Before You Leap

3.   Take Care of Yourself

4.   Reflect Before You Act

5.   Practice Acceptance and Empathy Rather than Judgment

6.   Take Responsibility Rather Than Blaming Others

7.   Forgive Rather than Taking Revenge

8.   Be Kind Instead of Being Cruel

9.   Communicate Lovingly Rather than Aggressively or Passively

10. Use Mistakes as Opportunities to Grow Instead of Reasons To
     Punish Yourself

11. Show Gratitude Whenever Possible

12. Observe and Change Irrational Beliefs and Destructive habits

13. Love Always Heals

We teach who we are. As we demonstrate these principles in our lives,
our children have a direct experience of them and absorb them into their
view of themselves and the world around them. When we speak in a
calm voice our children learn how to stay composed when provoked.
When we take responsibility for being late or acting inappropriately, we
teach our children the role they play in determining what their life looks
like at any particular moment. When we give our children positive feedback for a job well done, we are teaching them the power and self-
esteem that comes from being acknowledged.

MASTERFUL PARENTING

WHAT IT MEANS TO BE A MASTERFUL PARENT

- To realize that the primary task of parenting is to help our children to develop into self-sufficient adults. For this to occur, children must develop the positive self-concept, effective problem solving ability and self-discipline that social and emotional learning provide.

- To model what we want to teach. Understanding that children absorb not only the moral character but also the emotional maturity or immaturity of their parents.

- To choose kindness, by responding to situations in a manner that respects everyone's feelings.

- To understand and respect the developmental stage a child is going through.

- To recognize that our child's expression has value even if it is unlike our own.

- To realize that the type of communication used in the home has a profound effect on how our children will interact with others.

- To act as a guide and counselor for our children.

- To use conflicts with our children as a way to confront and resolve issues that we may have not dealt with.

- To realize the importance of setting boundaries.

- To realize the importance of positive feedback in creating self-esteem.

- To realize that in order to take care of our children, we must take better care of ourselves physically, emotionally, mentally and spiritually.

- To demonstrate acceptance, responsibility, conscious choice, empathy, forgiveness, effective listening and communication skills so that our children will learn and emulate these qualities.

GUIDE TO EFFECTIVELY USING THIS BOOK

Over the eleven years in which I've presented the Self-Mastery program, I have seen the lives of hundreds of parents transformed. My vision for this book is to inspire and help a wider audience to live a more rewarding life – a life in which serving ourselves and those we love and interact with becomes an ongoing commitment.

Whether you are enrolled in a Masterful Parenting Program or are reading this book without the benefit of classroom support, I cannot stress enough the importance of doing the home assignments. The exercises and home assignments will promote remarkable changes in your life and the lives of those around you, but again, you have to do them in order to reap the benefits. I suggest that you read one chapter at a time – ideally one per week – just as we do in the classroom. As you do the home assignments, it's a good idea to reread the chapter so that the material remains fresh in your mind. If possible, you should complete one full chapter, including the home assignment, before going on to the next chapter. How much effort you devote to this process is your choice, but I can tell you from experience that those participants who are really committed derive the greatest benefit.

Also, feel free to write your own notes and experiences in the margins.

THE COMMITMENT – GOING FOR MASTERY

As the Self-mastery program unfolds, I often hear participants exclaim, "This work is hard!" It is hard. It's easy to get angry, not listen and resist change. The quest for mastery can be frustrating, because you're observing and trying to transform patterns that have been reinforced over many years. For most of us, being judgmental or unforgiving has become second nature: it's not easy to accept and change that in ourselves. I encourage you to be gentle with yourself as you go through this journey. Be patient, but persevere. This book will help you to attain mastery over your life. That's a big project. It's bound to be an uphill battle at times.

But the rewards come in direct proportion to the effort and commitment that you invest. As you complete each step thoroughly, you'll see the results of what you've learned, in yourself and in your relationships with others, especially your children.

14

YOU ALWAYS HAVE A CHOICE

Masterful Parenting is a process of consciously choosing the most appropriate action in any given situation – the appropriate action being the one that provides the best possible experience for yourself and your children.

We are always making choices. Almost everything we think, do or say represents a choice. And, ideally everything we thought, did or said would provide the best possible outcome for ourselves and others. However, too often our choices are not choices at all, but unconscious reactions based on past conditioning or social pressures. Our parents, our teachers, our peers – even TV, movies and magazines – have all played their part in shaping our views of the world. We look at the world through an accumulation of attitudes, opinions and tastes imposed on us by outside influences. There is very little that we think, do or say, that isn't a direct result of our past conditioning.

We rarely view the world with the freshness and innocence of a young child. When someone leans over a baby's crib, the baby doesn't think, "What an ugly blouse," or "I don't like red curly hair," or "He's too fat." An infant's view of the world hasn't been tainted by judgments or comparisons.

Upon closer inspection, when we think we're making choices, often we are allowing our past conditioning and society's mores to choose for us. Who decided when it was suddenly fashionable for women to wear sneakers to work after a century of wearing high heels everyday? Who gave men permission to wear earrings when it was previously perceived as feminine? Who said that baggy pants and loose clothing were fashionable for boys when 30 years ago teenagers wore tight pants and pointy shoes? Did individuals decide, or did the media decide for us?

When we make a choice, we need to look at who or what is influencing our decision. I realized after practicing dentistry for several years that it did not suit my personality or talents. I had decided that I wanted to be a dentist at the ripe old age of thirteen. In reality, it was my parents, the influence of society and my Jewish culture which decided that dentistry would be a fine profession for me.

WHO IS IN CONTROL OF YOUR LIFE?

Most psychologists agree that the values and beliefs we absorb from our parents and teachers during the first seven years of life determine how we relate to ourselves and others for the rest of our lives. When we are children, our parents are like gods. We accept everything they say and do as Truth. When parents treat their children lovingly and make them feel valued, self-worth becomes the foundation of the child's development. If, on the other hand, children are denied love and attention during their formative years, the chances of them developing a healthy sense of self-esteem are greatly diminished.

Most negative attitudes and fears are created by painful memories from our early childhood experiences. Sexual abuse during childhood can manifest as sexual dysfunction. Fear of abandonment can become jealousy. A child's negative self-image is often the source of phobias, anorexia, obesity or substance abuse.

The deep limbic portion of our brain stores past emotional experiences. Whenever we remember a particular event, our brain releases chemicals similar to those released when we originally experienced the event. An example would be a rape victim who has an emotionally-based physical reaction whenever she sees a man who has a physical characteristic in common with her attacker. Similarly, people who had little bonding with their parents have a negative chemical imprint in their brain. Whenever someone looks at them the wrong way, it triggers the same chemical patterns in the brain as in the earlier negative experiences.

How do we overcome the effects of negative conditioning in ourselves? First, we have to acknowledge that past experience determines our present thoughts, attitudes, beliefs and fears. **Only when we acknowledge the influence of past conditioning can we develop the power to suspend those thoughts, attitudes, beliefs and fears.** The following story told by a Masterful Parenting participant illustrates this point:

"When I first began dating my wife, an incident occurred that dramatically influenced the course of our relationship. We were both feeling very loving towards each other when I said something to her in a joking manner. The next thing I knew, she hauled off and slapped me. Although it was not my intention, she thought that I was teasing her. After discussing the incident, she saw that my words triggered anger she'd felt but never expressed when, as a little girl, she was teased by her two older brothers."

Extreme emotional responses usually have very little to do with what is actually happening in the moment. If we look at ourselves honestly, we see that our out of balance emotions are almost always triggered by events from our past that we haven't yet resolved. Until we realize that we have a choice in the matter – that we can actually select our thoughts and the resultant behaviors through reflection and observation – we will inevitably rerun the same old patterns over and over again.

Let me give you a couple of examples from my own life. Several years ago I was involved in a lengthy process of buying an apartment. Whenever I heard my lawyer's voice on the answering machine, my first thought was to assume that something was wrong. I remained upset until I was able to speak with her and find out that nothing catastrophic had happened. In fact, she often had good news for me!

This tendency to expect the worst operated in many areas of my life. For example, if I had a dinner appointment with a friend and the friend left a message on my answering machine to call back, my first thought was that the dinner had been canceled. In these situations, my responses were as habitual and automatic as Pavlov's dog's and the emotions they evoked were quite painful.

17

I knew that negative thinking like this came from somewhere in my past. I had been unconsciously repeating this pattern for years. But once I began observing my fears and anxiety, I saw that I could choose to let go of the old pattern. Now when anxiety-provoking thoughts arise, I usually dismiss them as thoughts that don't serve me. Through self-awareness, I am better able to access information that more accurately reflects the reality of a current situation. As a result I feel much better about myself. I also do not experience the physical pain that often resulted from the negative thoughts and emotions.

FEELINGS FOLLOW THOUGHT

A man sees a snake lying on the ground at a distance in front of him. He becomes frightened and runs away screaming, "Snake! Snake!" Another man, who was observing the situation from a closer vantage point says, "Don't be afraid. That's not a snake. It's just a piece of rope lying on the ground." The first man's fear was real, though the snake was not. The feeling (fear) followed the thought (snake).

Every thought we have sends electrical signals through our brain. This, in turn, influences the limbic system (structures deep in our brains) which, depending upon the nature of the stimulation, translates our emotional state into a range of physical feelings of relaxation or tension. Dr. Mark George of the National Institute of Health determined that happy thoughts cool off the limbic system, whereas sad thoughts significantly increase deep limbic activity. Through this mechanism our thoughts significantly influence every cell in our bodies.

In other words, what we think determines what we feel. Anorexics get upset because they think that weighing 90 pounds is too fat. We get angry at someone's behavior because we think they **should know better.** We pace the floor when our son is 15 minutes late because we think that something horrible has happened to him. We react defensively when we think that our authority is being threatened.

Thinking positive thoughts cools down the limbic system and can lessen the irritability and depression caused by an overactive limbic structure. **Exercise is another, extremely effective, way to send blood to the deep limbic structures and calm the emotions.** In addition, protein has been proven essential for maintaining the health of the deep limbic structures. For this reason protein snacks, such as cheese or poultry, are usually preferable to sugary snacks, which can promote moodiness, lethargy and lack of focus.

STINKING THINKING

Given the thought-emotion connection, it would be a wonderful world if most of the thoughts we had were positive and thus produced a soothing emotional state. Unfortunately this is not the case. Researchers have measured that more than 70 percent of the thoughts we have are not beneficial to ourselves or others. Many of these negative thoughts are habitual and automatic. Moreover, not all thoughts are accurate or prove to be true when tested in reality. Thoughts that have the words "always, never, no one, everyone, everytime", etc. in them are usually not accurate. "He's always putting me down." "I'll never get a raise." "My children never listen to me." Such ideas are inaccurate, but nevertheless stimulate the limbic structure. Also, negative categories of thought such as focusing on the negative ("He probably will never call"), labeling yourself or someone else ("He's just a liar"), personalizing ("He seems angry, I must have done something wrong"), blaming ("I had nothing to do with the argument," "I couldn't help it," "It's all your fault") and worrying about the past or future stimulate the limbic structure and produce varying degrees of physical stress.

Most negative thoughts are habitual and go unnoticed. But even though they may not be noticed at a conscious level, they are taken in by our bodies in the form of physical tension. We will suffer the effects of our negative thoughts until we realize we have a choice: to be brought down by our own negativity or to move in a positive direction. While that all sounds very neat and simple in theory, how does it work in reality?

Let's say you have a habit of becoming angry and yelling when your spouse is emotionally upset and withdraws his or her affection. One day you come to a point where you begin **observing this process rather than reacting in a habitually negative manner.** With this new awareness, you understand that your spouse's emotional ups and downs don't necessarily have anything to do with you, are not your fault and certainly don't imply that your spouse is about to leave you. Once you have this understanding, you can try to identify why you tend to react the way you do. Reflecting on your childhood, you may notice a pattern whereby your parents led you to feel that you were to blame for their emotional upset. Or you may ask, "Who else, besides my spouse, has made me feel badly when they were out of balance?" Or, "When did I associate someone being upset with me implied that they were going to leave me?"

Think about the times you've reacted with anger to someone else's emotional imbalance. Did your reaction ever do any good? Probably not. Probably never. So try an experiment. The next time a loved one gets upset, try to react with empathy rather than anger. See whether it makes a difference. And if a week later your loved one becomes moody and the same old pattern kicks in – you get angry and yell – don't despair and beat up on yourself. Just be aware of your reaction and resolve to do things differently the next time.

DON'T BE CRUEL

We can consciously choose our response to every situation that is presented. Yet, because it has become a habit, responding emotionally is much easier than reflecting and consciously choosing:

- It's easy to not pay attention, hard to really listen to others.

- It's easy to judge, hard to accept.

- It's easy to hate, hard to forgive.

- It's often easy to communicate passively or aggressively, hard to be assertive.

Unfortunately, we often suffer because these unconscious reactions don't often produce what is best for ourselves and others.

Again, no one ever said this was easy. This path is not founded on feeling comfortable. It's foundation is leading a life where we do what is best for ourselves and others. If you are in doubt as to whether you are best serving yourself and others, go with the kindest of action. This approach also applies to how we treat ourselves.

As you continue reading, you will be presented with responses to life's challenges that you may never have considered. In time, you will naturally and consistently act from a position of wisdom and compassion when facing a specific stressful situation. But it may take a while before you get there. How soon depends on the understanding you have embodied, how much suffering you are willing to endure before changing and an unknown variable called Grace. Grace is simply knowing that behavior changes at the exact moment it is supposed to change. This knowledge provides us with patience and acceptance for ourselves and those who are important to us.

HOW DO YOU MAKE YOURSELF MISERABLE EXERCISE

Do the following exercise, then allow yourself one week to complete the home assignment. Reread the chapter as often as necessary.

I. MAKE A LIST OF THINGS YOU DO THAT MAKE YOU MISERABLE. For example:

- Eating too much junk food
- Saying negative things about yourself to yourself
- Arguing
- Not asking for what you want
- Not getting enough sleep

2. **FOR EACH ITEM ON YOUR LIST SUGGEST SOMETHING ELSE THAT YOU COULD DO IN ORDER TO AVOID BECOMING MISERABLE.** For example:

- Instead of eating junk food, you could eat fruit.

- Instead of feeling bad about yourself, you could reflect and choose a more supportive inner dialogue.

- Instead of arguing you could allow five uninterrupted minutes for each person to explain their point of view.

- Instead of not asking for what you want, you could make a list and move through your passiveness by asking for what you want at the appropriate moment.

- Instead of not getting enough sleep, you could turn the TV off earlier every evening.

22

YOU ALWAYS HAVE A CHOICE

1. REFLECTING ON YOUR PAST, WRITE DOWN THE MOST SIGNIFICANT CHOICES YOU HAVE MADE IN YOUR LIFE. FOR EXAMPLE: STOPPING SMOKING, MOVING, GETTING MARRIED, HAVING KIDS, ETC.

   Stopped smoking
   got married
   had kids

   became special needs advocate after childrens' diagnoses

2. CHOOSE ONE ITEM FROM YOUR "HOW YOU MAKE YOURSELF MISERABLE" LIST AND USE THE JOURNAL FORMAT BELOW TO RECORD THE RESULTS OF A NEW CHOICE YOU MADE.

   23

   Journal format

   - Describe the situation. *lack of sleep*

   - How do you usually respond to the situation? *Try to go to bed earlier*

   - List some alternative responses.

   - What happened when new responses were used compared to the habitual ones?

   - What have you learned?

3. DURING THE WEEK KEEP A DAILY RECORD OF SITUATIONS IN WHICH, BY CHOOSING A DIFFERENT RESPONSE FROM YOUR HABITUAL ONE, YOU SAW POSITIVE CHANGES. Be open to the possibilities that new choices can bring.

PARTICIPANTS' COMMENTS

These comments are included to give you some idea of what other parents, teachers and students have experienced. When applicable, they can provide valuable insight regarding issues you may be dealing with in your own life. Again, I ask you to be open to the possibilities that new choices can bring.

- A woman shared her emotional pain about being unable to hug or even lovingly touch her 14-year-old daughter. She also realized how much her inability to show affection upset her daughter. She said that she just did not feel natural being affectionate. My suggestion was that she should reach out and do it even though it didn't feel natural. She tried it and commented, "At first I felt a little phony and unnatural. After reaching out several times, it became a lot easier and I actually started to enjoy being affectionate with my daughter."

- A mother complained that she couldn't stand it when her husband and 13-year-old daughter constantly argued with each other. She would listen for a while, but inevitably she would get upset and yell at them both for fighting. The class pointed out that maybe this wasn't her battle and that the problem her husband and daughter were having was their problem to work out. When she was asked, "Does your intervention do any good?" she sighed and said, "No." The new choice she shared in her homework was to leave the house and go rollerskating whenever their arguing started getting to her. She reported that this choice was really working for her because the frequency of their arguing decreased, since it appears that her husband and daughter missed her presence when she would leave the house.

- A ninth grade English teacher felt miserable because upon arriving home each day after work, she was responsible for everything that her three children needed. Her husband would come home from a day's work and read the paper or sit and watch TV. She recalled,

"One day I made the choice to tell him that he was not free to just sit on the couch and read the paper when he came home. I'm lucky that my husband is very understanding and after I spoke up, he now assists with taking care of the kids."

- A wonderful parent stated, "I used to constantly argue with my husband about anything and everything. Over the weeks, I have learned that when he says something that annoys me, I can just listen and not argue. At first he didn't know how to react. My lack of response just made him angrier. But recently he has gotten a lot lighter with his requests and conversations with me. I feel better about him and I know he feels better about himself – and me, I hope."

- After working on the destructive habit of saying "yes" when she wanted to say "no," a teacher responded, "Sometimes I feel I may hurt someone's feelings if I say no. But when I say yes when I really want to say no, I could kick myself. I get angry at myself and at the person I said yes to. Of course I never tell them or let them know I am angry. Sometimes I feel used, even though I know it was my choice to say yes. After reading the assignment, I decided that if the situation arose again, I would say what I really wanted to say. There were two times last week when something was asked of me where I felt it was expected that I say yes. I told both people no. Even though they both seemed annoyed, I felt better about my choices. I didn't have any turmoil within me about what I should or should not have said. I didn't feel as if I was doing something that I didn't want to do, either."

- A mother was upset because her eight year old son, a great artist, was the "class clown" who was always seeking approval from his classmates.

    Another parent suggested, "My son was very much like yours at that age. After several attempts at counseling produced very little resolution, I decided to enroll him in an after school arts program. Almost overnight he became more confident and less needy around his peers."

Discovering an effective approach often requires creativity, persistence and the humility to ask others for help.

- A mother bought her 13-year-old daughter a pair of boots she really wanted. The girl wasn't doing her chores. Instead of fighting with her daughter, she put the boots on a table so the girl could see them. She told the girl if she did her chores every day for the next week, she could have the boots. It worked.

Note: Some of you may be offended by a parent paying their child to do chores. Let's be realistic: We all work for some form of reward. Rather than arguing philosophy, I am more concerned with making choices that work for a particular person in a specific situation.

2

WHO'S REALLY LISTENING?

Focused listening is the essence of communication and the first step to being a masterful parent.

We have all been told that in order to be good parents, we must learn how to effectively communicate with our children. We take this advice to heart and try very hard to find ways to clearly express our thoughts and feelings, state our opinions and offer advice. The problem with this approach, however, is that the kind of communication we seek, the real "meeting of the minds" that we want, does not begin with talking – it begins with listening, really listening. Countless hours are spent teaching us how to speak and express ourselves. But how many of us were taught how to **really listen**? **We really listen to our children so we can understand how they see the world and better respond to their needs.**

The importance of listening becomes more profound when we consider that 55 percent of what is communicated occurs through body language, 38 percent with tone of voice and only 7 percent through what is said. In order to listen, really listen, and access all the factual, emotional and psychological information that is available in any communication, we need to quiet our minds. We need to turn off the play-by-play commentator, resist the snap judgments and listen.

QUIET PLEASE

Do you experience a place inside of you that is quiet? A place where there is just silence? Is there a place in your mind where there is no chatter? You do not have to experience this place all or most of the time to answer yes. Let's make it even easier. You can answer yes if you just believe that such quietness exists. For those of you who have never experienced quietness of mind and think that it can only occur after a lobotomy, I have an exercise for you:

- Reread the first paragraph of this chapter again. (I'm trusting you, please don't let me down.)

- Read it another time and note whether you were having any distracting thoughts at the same time you were reading the material.

- Read the section again and whatever thoughts come to mind, let them go and come back to just reading the material.

Now let's talk about what you just experienced. When you were taking in the information on the page, a part of you was quiet. In these moments when your mind was still, you were just receiving the information – nothing else.

Were you able to experience this quietness? I hope so. You must be quiet inside in order to really focus and pay attention. When you were thinking about what the words meant, judging my instructions or thinking about whether you had paid the phone bill, you were doing something other than focusing on the first paragraph. **It's a matter of choosing where you focus your attention.** Are you focusing on the words on the page or on your thoughts?

I WANT TO BE LIKE MIKE

When basketball superstar Michael Jordan is driving to the hoop and is just about to stuff the ball, do you think he is thinking about how his muscles are working, how fast he's moving, how hard he's breathing, or what's for dinner? Or is he instinctively moving in for the score?

Think about dancing. Doesn't it feel wonderful when the music flows into you and moves your body? What would your dancing look like if your mind chattered, "OK, now raise the left leg two inches, set it down, put weight on it while swinging the right leg three inches?" or "I wonder if

I'm doing this right?" Have you ever seen anyone dance awkwardly? This is the result of an active mind participating where it doesn't belong.

Masterful listening requires a quiet, receptive mind. **When you are practicing masterful listening – the kind of listening that can really make a difference – you are simply being receptive to what the other person is saying. Nothing else.** Sometimes parents tell me, "I can wash the dishes, talk on the phone and still listen to my kid." This is not focused, masterful listening. This is washing the dishes, talking on the phone and half-heartedly listening.

THE TOP THIRTEEN THINGS WE DO INSTEAD OF REALLY LISTENING

1. We think about a solution to the other person's problem before they have finished.

2. We assume the other person doesn't know what they are talking about.

3. We space out. Because of boredom, restlessness or our own short attention span, we start to think about something completely unrelated.

4. We react to one part of what the other person is saying and interrupt, evaluate, probe or advise instead of listening.

5. We internally rehearse our response while the other person is still speaking.

6. We worry about what the person is thinking about us.

7. We become annoyed and impatient with the other person's pace or accent.

8. We **do** something else while listening.

9. We react defensively to what is said by getting angry or shutting down.

10. We try to identify with the speaker by telling our own story.

11. We try to listen when we are emotionally out of balance or physically exhausted.

12. We judge the person who's speaking. This includes judging people's clothes, appearance or manner, and indulging any prejudice that prevents real listening.

13. We are attached to our own point of view and are not totally open to what is being said.

Parents are often confused when I suggest to them that offering a solution is not listening. They often say, "Isn't it my job as a parent to provide guidance?" We're not really listening when we think about a solution at the same time someone is discussing an issue. The result is more beneficial when we listen first, totally take it all in, and then allow our inner wisdom to come forward with an appropriate response. The process becomes a dance of receiving and responding.

Sometimes, when we share a problem, we're not really looking for a solution – just someone to listen. When you have a problem, you may call a friend just to "talk" – not to get "fixed." Kids are the same way; often they're not looking for a particular answer. They just want you to listen.

How often have you found yourself trying to reason with your children, presenting them with what you know is a practical solution, only to see it all fall on deaf ears because they have already taken a position and dug in? We often end up in a showdown where an endless argument ensues and the child is forced to do something against his or her will or stomps off in disgust. **Masterful listening can create a safe, loving and caring environment where you can drop rather than defend a position.** Often, your child will feel honored and empowered simply because you have taken the time to listen. It is from this empowered position that they can find their own answers.

HOW DEEP CAN LISTENING GO?

When we practice masterful listening we are experiencing more than just hearing the other person's voice. We understand who we are dealing with not only by their words but also by how we feel inside while engaged in the conversation. We actually "feel" and "intuit" the other person's intentions, emotions, needs and fears. The tone, the nuances, the body language and the facial expressions are all ways we come to know this person. The deeper we listen, the more information is available to us and the better we can understand the other person's point of view.

An example of the depth that listening can reach was poignantly demonstrated in a research project. Sometimes when I use this example, workshop participants get upset. I hope you understand the spirit of the research and the learning that it reveals.

A mother rabbit was placed on a beach and wired with a heart monitor. Her babies were put on a boat and taken five miles out to sea and sacrificed. At the very moment the bunnies were killed, the mother's heart rate changed dramatically. Even though they were five miles away, her body perceived what was going on with her babies. This phenomenon can be categorized as listening at a very deep level – a level that involves intuition and feeling. Mothers often report instances of knowing what is happening with their children even though they are not physically with them. **When the mind is quiet, when you are able to stop the chattering, a whole new world of possibilities opens.**

PUTTING MASTERFUL LISTENING INTO PRACTICE

Now, let's put masterful listening into practice. This lesson means very little unless you are willing to do each home assignment. The more committed you are, the more benefits you will receive. So here's another opportunity to live more of your potential.

MASTERFUL LISTENING

Over the next seven days, observe what it is like to practice listening to your child and record the specifics of at least one communication per day. A family member, friend or co-worker can be used for this exercise if it is not possible to work with your child. You can also use more than one person over the seven day period. Write down the answers to the following questions (I suggest you use the worksheet that follows the questions):

1. **WHAT DID YOUR CHILD SAY?** Be brief. Simply record the general topic of conversation; for example, "We spoke about her wanting new shoes" or "She told me about her problems with a teacher." There is no need to give a word-by-word account.

2. **DID YOU DO ANYTHING INSTEAD OF LISTENING?** Did you practice masterful listening or were you distracted? Please be honest! If necessary, refer back to the Top Thirteen List.

3. **WHAT EMOTIONS OR FEELINGS DID YOU EXPERIENCE DURING YOUR CONVERSATION?** Be specific. For example: "I experienced anger, boredom, surprise, disappointment, etc."

4. **DID YOU EXPERIENCE YOUR CHILD OR THE SITUATION IN A DIFFERENT WAY WHEN YOU PRACTICED MASTERFUL LISTENING?** For example: "I thought my child was being disrespectful, but I came to realize that he was just confused."

I HAVE ALWAYS HATED HOMEWORK

The top six excuses for not doing the listening homework

My child lost his voice.
I lost my hearing for a week.
My child ran away from home.
I ran away from home.
I totally forgot there was homework.

The single biggest reason for doing the listening homework

Research has shown that we learn and retain:

10% of what we hear
15% of what we see
20% of what we see and hear
40% of what we discuss with others
80% of what we experience directly and practice (e.g., homework)
90% of what we attempt to teach others

TIPS FOR MASTERFUL LISTENING

- Be willing to listen without doing something else at the same time.

- Accept the other person.

- Respect that all human beings are valuable. We may not agree with what they have to say, but they have a right to say what is true for them.

- Acknowledge that every person has the capacity to solve their own problems (we don't have to "fix" them).

- Create adequate time to listen.

- Realize that the goal of listening is to understand the other person.

WE TEACH WHO WE ARE – NOT WHAT WE KNOW

34

LISTENING HOMEWORK WORKSHEET

DAY ONE

1.   *Topic of communication*

2.   *What did you do instead of listening?*

3.   *Emotions that you experienced*

4.   *Realizations that occurred from doing the exercise*

LISTENING HOMEWORK WORKSHEET

DAY TWO

1.   Topic of communication

2.   What did you do instead of listening?

3.   Emotions that you experienced

4.   Realizations that occurred from doing the exercise

LISTENING HOMEWORK WORKSHEET

DAY THREE

1.   *Topic of communication*

2.   *What did you do instead of listening?*

3.   *Emotions that you experienced*

4.   *Realizations that occurred from doing the exercise*

LISTENING HOMEWORK WORKSHEET

DAY FOUR

1.   *Topic of communication*

2.   *What did you do instead of listening?*

3.   *Emotions that you experienced*

4.   *Realizations that occurred from doing the exercise*

LISTENING HOMEWORK WORKSHEET

DAY FIVE

1.   *Topic of communication*

2.   *What did you do instead of listening?*

3.   *Emotions that you experienced*

4.   *Realizations that occurred from doing the exercise*

LISTENING HOMEWORK WORKSHEET

DAY SIX

1.   *Topic of communication*

2.   *What did you do instead of listening?*

3.   *Emotions that you experienced*

4.   *Realizations that occurred from doing the exercise*

LISTENING HOMEWORK WORKSHEET

DAY SEVEN

1.   *Topic of communication*

2.   *What did you do instead of listening?*

3.   *Emotions that you experienced*

4.   *Realizations that occurred from doing the exercise*

PARTICIPANTS' COMMENTS

- A mother of a 14-year-old responded, "I never understood what the teachers meant when they said my daughter was so sweet. Last night when I really listened to my daughter and didn't try to interject my 'I-know-better' point of view, I experienced what her teachers were talking about."

- A mother of three reported, "I used to talk and listen to all three kids at once. What I did differently as a result of this listening assignment was take time in a private space and listen to one child at a time. I was amazed at how much each one opened up and how they shared information about themselves that I never knew before."

- "After the listening class I realized that there was a wiseguy student that I was not listening to. Every time he opened his mouth, I pre-judged what he was going to say and basically turned myself off. This week I listened to what he had to say and although there was some silliness, there were also things that he said that were very important to hear."

- I found this fourth grade teacher's "listening" experience to be very profound: "A student explained that she was often late because she doesn't have an alarm clock and her mother wakes her up late. I noticed that while she was speaking I felt upset and at the same time, I was trying to find a solution to her dilemma. I saw for the first time that this is what I normally do – solve a problem rather then use masterful listening.

  "The next day I went up to her and asked her what was wrong. I asked if it was hard for her to get up in the morning and if she went to bed late. She simply said that she didn't like coming to school because she felt dumb because she had been left back last year. I let her speak and carefully listened which helped me realize that her lateness did not stem from laziness but from insecurities and lack of motivation."

- An eighth grader observed, "When I listened instead of spacing out or wanting to be right, I realized that the reason my mother wanted me to be home by 9:00 was that she cared and was concerned for my safety."

- Another mother said, "In the past, I usually didn't pay much attention to what my eight-year-old daughter had to say. But when I listened to her, she started telling me things about herself that I never knew before. Some of these things weren't pleasant to hear. She told me she felt that I didn't love her as much as I loved her younger sister. I never realized she felt this way. As a result of listening, I was able to tell her that I loved her just as much as I love her sister. I learned that people open up when we give them the space to open up."

- Another parent commented, "My husband is telling me about his job. Some of his deals have fallen through. I don't respond. I hear him repeating the same thing over and over, 'I got to make money, I got to make money.' I don't react or question him. What I hear for the first time is his frustration with the rate of progress he's making and his concerns about paying for our upcoming vacation. Today, I'm not angry with him for being preoccupied. I think maybe I understand him more because I listened."

- A fellow teacher came to me asking for advice regarding how to finish her Master's degree. I was able to give her my undivided attention as she spoke about how her responsibilities at home, work and school were interfering with her education. As I was listening, she was able to find a way to schedule her time so she could complete her schooling. She thanked me for just listening.

Masterful listening is not something you do only with your children. As you practice listening and become more and more aware of what you do instead of listening, you will find that this skill applies to every relationship in your life. What you do instead of listening may depend on whether you are communicating with your child, spouse or work colleague, but I promise, if you become a better listener, your relationships will improve.

44

3

TAKE CARE OF YOURSELF SO
YOU CAN HELP TAKE CARE OF OTHERS

Being a masterful parent requires the ability to take care of our-
selves so we can better nurture our children.

In our desire to be good parents and take care of our children, we often
forget to take care of ourselves. Between making sure that our children
are fed, clothed, off to school on time, and given supportive direction, it
seems almost impossible to find any time for ourselves.

When we become parents, we do not stop being human beings –
people with natural needs that must be acknowledged. Even though it
may be fun to be with our children, we still need to socialize with our
peers. **In order to be balanced and whole, we also need time to reflect,
relax and experience peace.**

Many of us believe that, as parents, it is selfish to take care of ourselves. The truth is that taking care of ourselves enables us to better
serve our children. When we care for ourselves, we also show our children what self-nurturing looks like, which is among the most valuable
lessons we can teach them.

PRACTICAL WAYS OF TAKING CARE OF OURSELVES

In order to take better care of ourselves, we need to be nurtured on four
basic levels: the physical, the emotional, the mental and the spiritual.

On a **physical** level, it is obvious that if we become ill or rundown, it
is extremely difficult to function effectively. Regular exercise, sound
nutrition and adequate rest positively influence our quality of life on
every level.

On an **emotional** level, if we are upset about something that happens at work or with our spouse or a friend and we don't deal with it appropriately, the discord often spills over into our interaction with our children. Relationships thrive when we accept, understand and effectively communicate our feelings.

On a **mental** level, boredom, routine and lack of stimulation produce frustration and rob us of vitality. Reading, expanding our professional knowledge, being with interesting people and learning new things are important ways to enrich our lives.

On a **spiritual** level, if we feel lost, hopeless and in despair, it becomes difficult for our children to be inspired. Trust in one's own worth and the basic goodness of life opens the door to Grace.

The following are ways we can better take care of ourselves:

PHYSICAL
Exercising
Eating better
Relaxing
Meditating
Sharing the care of your children with family or other trusted people
Getting your hair done; having a manicure
Taking a vacation
Taking time for an enjoyable hobby or craft

EMOTIONAL
Calling a friend just to talk about what's going on in your life
Expressing needs
Listening to music
Having a social life
Giving and receiving affection (animals count!)

MENTAL
Taking courses

Reading a book
Exploring an idea for a project
Following up on plans for further education
Reading and completing the exercises in this book

SPIRITUAL
Taking time out for prayer, meditation or other religious practices
Making a commitment to personal growth
Writing in a journal
Reading material from spiritual teachers
Sending positive thoughts to someone who is ill or unhappy
Spending time with uplifting people
Helping others
Practicing humility, gratitude and compassion

Many of these suggestions have benefits on more than one level. For instance, after exercising, we not only feel better physically, but are often more balanced emotionally and mentally as well. Another example would be the way in which the foods we eat can affect our physical and emotional well being as well as our state of mind. Time and time again I have observed that certain foods have a negative emotional effect. I always think, "This time it will be different." But sure enough, almost every time after eating sugar I become mentally unfocused or seem to get upset by a circumstance that usually wouldn't upset me. For many of us, the foods that have the greatest likelihood of unbalancing us by producing an allergic reaction are: sugar, wheat, dairy and soy products.

When we meditate we feel mentally alert, physically renewed and emotionally calmed as well as spiritually uplifted. During meditation we stop for a period of time and observe rather than get carried away by the moment-to-moment activity of our mind, emotions and body. We slow down and become aware of the ongoing, habitual and unproductive nature of most of our thoughts. Also, as a result of meditation, we tend to more naturally make choices that serve ourselves and others. It's as if we don't have to think about the right thing to do. Meditation places us directly in the flow of what is appropriate for ourselves and others. The **social and emotional educational methods presented in this book, coupled with meditation and exercise, are very powerful tools in changing habitual patterns of thought and behavior that do not serve us.**

THE IMPORTANCE OF RELAXATION

Everybody has a different way of nurturing and taking care of themselves. One of the most effective and often neglected ways of nurturing ourselves involves periodic relaxation. Listen to this mother of six: "For years, from the moment I woke up to get my kids ready for school till I went to bed after midnight, I took no time to relax. Then, about a year ago, I decided that my parenting would improve if I first took better care of myself. So every day, no matter what, I lock myself in the bathroom for a minimum of 20 minutes to take a relaxing bath. Instead of being frazzled, I become recharged and able to more effectively deal with the kids."

OUR CHILDREN ALSO DESERVE A BREAK TODAY

Our children are confronted with the realities of AIDS, weapons possession, suicide, violence in the media, terrorism, drug and alcohol abuse – challenges few of us encountered when we were growing up. A study assessing the emotional well-being of seven-to fourteen-year-old American children emphatically illustrates this observation. Done first in the mid-1970s, then repeated with similar youngsters 15 years later, the survey found that, on average, the basic indicators of emotional health for America's children had declined across the board. They were more impulsive, disobedient, anxious, fearful, lonely and sad. Children's scores declined on 42 such indicators and improved on none of them over the 15-year period. There were also significant increases in the frequency of teen violence, suicide, rape and the number of weapons-related crimes.

We need to demonstrate more empathy for our children. We can nurture them by encouraging them to engage in stress-reducing activities such as physical recreation and relaxation. Many of the other suggestions mentioned for taking care of ourselves can also be applied to our children.

"NOBODY IS GOING TO GIVE YOU WHAT YOU DON'T THINK YOU DESERVE"

In class, I often quote sayings and share stories that were told to me by teachers. But one time, an original, honest-to-goodness quote came out of my mouth: "Nobody is going to give you what you don't think you deserve." I've been thinking more and more deeply about this ever since I first said it. I believe that at a deep level we have created our present finances, relationships and life styles because they are what we think we deserve. Let me give you an example: I asked my class of senior high school students, "How much money would you like to make once you are established in the world?" One student responded, "$45,000 a year." Another student said, "$250,000 a year." I asked the second student what his father did. "My father is part owner of the King Ranch," he said, "on the island of Hawaii."

Having lived in Hawaii, I knew that the King Ranch was not only the largest ranch there, but in the entire United States as well. For this student $250,000 was not a lot of money, whereas $45,000 was a lot of money for the first student. These two students were similar ethically and academically. It was their different socioeconomic backgrounds that influenced their financial expectations.

When we begin taking total responsibility for what we think we deserve, we can begin the process of functioning on a more fulfilling level physically, emotionally, mentally and spiritually. This process of change begins with looking at the source of the beliefs we have about our capacity or our right to manifest our full potential at every level. This can lead to a profound consideration of the limitless possibilities that are available to us as human beings, leading to meaningful actions that bring these possibilities into reality. This idea was beautifully expressed in Nelson Mandela's 1994 Inaugural Address where he quoted a statement attributed to Marianne Williamson:

> "Our worst fear is not that we are inadequate. Our deepest fear is that we are powerful beyond measure. It is our light not our darkness that most frightens us. We ask ourselves, who am I to be brilliant, gorgeous, talented and fabulous? Actually, who are you not to be? You are a child of God. Your playing small doesn't serve the world. There is nothing enlightened about shrinking so that others don't feel insecure around you. We were born to make manifest the glory of God within us. It is in everyone and as we let our own light shine, we unconsciously give other people permission to do the same. As we are liberated from our fear, our presence automatically liberates others."

TAKING CARE OF YOURSELF

1. **EVERY DAY FOR THE NEXT WEEK, DO SOMETHING NICE FOR YOURSELF (ON A PHYSICAL, EMOTIONAL, MENTAL OR SPIRITUAL LEVEL) THAT YOU DON'T USUALLY DO.** Make it simple and practical. For instance, it may be more realistic for you to walk for ten minutes each day rather than running three miles.

2. **EVERY DAY FOR THE NEXT WEEK, FREEFORM WRITE AT LEAST TWO PAGES (FRONT AND BACK SIDE IS ONE PAGE).** Freeform writing is a technique that enables you to let go of emotional and mental tension. It is done by sitting down in a quiet area and writing down whatever comes to your mind. Just write down whatever you are thinking without changing it in any way. For example: "I'm bored, tired, cooking, noise sound what are they up to." The whole exercise usually takes about ten minutes. After this is completed, it is important that you do not reread what you wrote, but instead rip up the paper, burn it or flush it away. This can be a very powerful exercise. I receive the most benefit from this exercise when I do it first thing in the morning or after a stressful day.

3. **EACH DAY, ACKNOWLEDGE TO YOURSELF THAT YOU ARE DOING THE BEST YOU CAN AND THAT YOU HAVE YOUR CHILDREN'S BEST INTEREST AT HEART. YOU MIGHT WANT TO LIST THE SPECIFIC WAYS IN WHICH YOU ARE A GOOD PARENT.** (For example, you shop, clean, express affection, check your child's homework, etc.) It sounds simple, but just try it!

4. **IF YOU HAVE THE RELAXATION TAPE, THIS IS A GOOD TIME TO BEGIN LISTENING TO IT.**

51

PARTICIPANTS' COMMENTS

- One mother responded, "Last week was the first time in years that I went out and had lunch by myself. It might not sound like a big deal, but when you eat practically every meal with your two young sons, it really is a pleasure to enjoy a quiet meal alone."

- Another mother said, "I followed your suggestion and twice last week I locked myself in the bathroom and took a 20 minute bubble bath. At one point my six-year-old started banging on the door and I explained to him that this was my 'time out' and that I would play with him when I was done. After a minute or two of crying, he went into his room and occupied himself."

- A teacher shared, "I used to routinely eat the school lunches and I noticed that after lunch I was tired and irritable. I decided to bring salads and home cooked food each day for lunch. I was delighted to see that my energy level does not drop anymore after eating."

- Another mother responded, "I really did something different. Six years ago, before we had our daughter, my husband and I used to love to go out dancing. Last Saturday night, we splurged. We got a baby-sitter and went out to a club and danced until two in the morning."

- A parent responded, "The thing that usually makes me the most miserable is my weight. Growing up I was always thin but after giving birth to my third child, it has been very difficult to take off the extra seven to ten pounds. I sometimes deal with this in a negative way by eating anything I want because I say to myself, 'What difference does it make if I am overweight?' I have begun to deal with it in a positive way by watching what I eat and exercising four times this week."

4

REFLECTION BEFORE ACTION & HOW YOU RELATE TO THE ISSUE IS THE ISSUE

The development of reflection and considering the consequences before taking action not only transforms behavior, but also is the true source of self-knowledge, creative problem-solving and self-esteem.

In my workshops, I ask my students, "You're driving down the street and someone cuts you off. What choices do you have?"

Typical responses include: "I'd yell at them..." "I'd swear under my breath..." "I'd cut them off..." "Ignore them and just drive on..."

Then I ask, "What are the consequences of each of these responses?" (You can answer this for yourself.)

One day, while walking on 14th Street in New York City, I saw a man driving a convertible sports car with a woman seated next to him. Behind them were two men in a SUV. The men in the SUV had beeped the horn a couple of times to encourage the man in the sports car to speed up. When they stopped at a light, the man driving the sports car grabbed his Club locking device, walked over to the SUV and smashed every window in the vehicle. (I know many of you think this is a typical occurrence in New York City but, trust me, it isn't.) Think about the consequences of this response on all the concerned parties.

Along the same lines, I'll ask my teenage students, "You sit down in the cafeteria. Unexpectedly, you see that you're right next to someone you know that has been talking about you behind your back. What do you do?"

The usual responses include: "I'd hit him..." "I'd yell at him..." "I'd ignore him..." "I'd talk to him and see if it is true..." "I'd move my seat..."

Then I ask, "What are the consequences of each of these responses?" This is the important question each of us needs to continuously ask ourselves throughout the day.

OF MICE AND MEN

Years ago, a teacher of mine told me a wonderful story that relates to reflection and action:

"You know, people are just like rats. The only difference is that rats are smarter. Let me give you an example. You take a piece of cheese and put it at the end of a maze. You take a rat and put him behind a gate at the beginning of the maze. When you open the gate, the rat will go through the maze, eat the cheese and return to where he started. Every time you open the gate, the same course of events occurs: the rat goes through the maze, eats the cheese and returns. The fifth time you open the gate, you take away the cheese. The rat goes through the maze, finds no cheese and returns. You open the gate and again take away the cheese. The rat will again negotiate the maze, find no cheese and return. The third time you provide no cheese and open the gate, however, the rat will just stand there and not bother to go through the maze. Rats are like people. The only difference is that rats are smarter. The rat knows to stop a certain behavior when there is no cheese. Humans keep doing the same thing over and over and over, expecting cheese long after they should have realized that there is no cheese to be had."

How many times have we eaten food that over and over has made us feel bad and convinced ourselves that this time it would be different? Or instead of something you have eaten, how about something that's eating you? How about a relationship that just doesn't work? Have you noticed how we often pick the same person (but with a different name and shoe size) as the one that made us miserable, expecting that "this one will be different"?

To expect different results from the same actions or series of actions is one definition of insanity.

HOW YOU RELATE TO THE ISSUE IS THE ISSUE

A woman has just cooked breakfast for her husband (reverse the gender roles if you like.) After eating, he walks out the door saying, "See ya later."

She shouts after him, "See ya later? What do you mean, see ya later? Every day I cook for you. I get up every morning and make the coffee, toast the bread, scramble the eggs, set the table, clean up and wash the dishes and you leave – and all you can say is, 'See ya later'."

He responds, "There'd be no food to cook if I didn't go to work every day while you just stay home." "Oh yeah?" she responds, "You try it! You see how easy it is staying home with these kids everyday!"

We'll leave the rest of the discussion to your imagination. Now the apparent issue here is that two people have just had a fight and have gone off angry at each other. **But the real issue is not the fight – it's how they're going to relate to the fight.** Let's look at positive and negative choices people make when relating to issues. Negative ways include: worrying, sleeping, denial, getting even, violence, eating, smoking, drugs, alcohol and staring at the TV. Many people use negative habits in order to avoid dealing with life's problems.

Positive ways of dealing with being upset include relaxing, taking a hot bath, reading, enjoying a hobby, crying, meditating, talking to a friend or counselor, exercising and discussing the problem with the appropriate person. Positive solutions usually incorporate aspects of acceptance, communication, forgiveness, self respect and respect for others.

The quality of our life changes when we take time to reflect and make positive choices that lift ourselves and others out of pain and into healing.

DON'T BE IN SUCH A HURRY TO WORRY

Inevitably, whenever we discuss How You Relate To the Issue Is the Issue, the topic of worrying comes up. When used constructively, worrying motivates us to take appropriate action. For instance, your 12-year-old daughter says she'll return from a friend's house by 5:00 p.m. It's now 5:30 and you begin to worry. After a short while you call the friend's house in order to find out your daughter's whereabouts. At its best, worrying is a call to action.

In contrast, let's say you have an important job interview coming up in two days. You observe that you are beginning to worry incessantly. You know that you have taken every step you could to be prepared for the interview, e.g. picked out the right clothes, found out as much as you could about the company, arranged for transportation, etc. At this point, because there is nothing left to do, worrying only serves to make you miserable.

Parents often protest, "It's only because I care that I worry. If I didn't care, I wouldn't even think of worrying." My experience is that when we care, there are other positive choices available to us. After the appropriate action is taken, does the act of worrying do anything for you or the other person besides making you sick?

Let me reinforce this notion with another example: When I ask a group of parents, "What do you worry about?" frequently I get the response, "I worry about my child's safety going to and from school."

Your child is walking home after school and you are sitting home worrying. Are you making your child safer by worrying? Are you doing anything to help your child by worrying? I suspect the answer to both of these questions is "no".

So I ask, "What constructive action could you take in this situation?" (I did have several parents say that instead of worrying, they drive their child to and from school each day. This is a great solution but inappropriate or impractical for most of us.)

Another possibility we came up with in class was to picture your child surrounded by God's protective light, with a smile on her face, safely walking home from school. Does this choice hurt you? Does this choice hurt your child? At worst, it doesn't hurt her, and at best it may help her. Remember the rabbits from earlier on? Energy can be projected out from beyond our bodies and affect others. Many parents have reported that this choice works a lot better than worrying.

Before you do the following home assignment, I would like to mention one more helpful observation regarding the nature of worrying. Many of us want to control the way things are. **Worrying is an expression of the fear that comes from not being in control of a situation.**

From early infancy we teach our children values and what we believe to be the correct way to respond to life's challenges. There comes a point when our children know what we expect of them. Still, they are going to do what they are going to do. Worrying represents the fear that what they are going to do is what we don't want them to do. **In reality, when our 15-year-old walks out the door and takes on the day, we have no control over him or her.**

57

HOW YOU RELATE TO THE ISSUE IS THE ISSUE

1. **TO UNDERSTAND THE REAL NATURE OF WORRYING AND ITS FUTILITY, SIT DOWN FOR TEN MINUTES AND DO NOTHING ELSE BUT WORRY ABOUT WHAT YOU USUALLY WORRY ABOUT.** Could you last the full ten minutes? Now for the rest of the day don't dwell on any worrying thoughts that enter your mind. Instead, make an agreement with yourself to dwell on these thoughts in your next ten minute worrying session. Repeat this exercise each day for one week.

2. **PICK ONE AREA OF YOUR LIFE THAT YOU TEND TO WORRY ABOUT HABITUALLY.** Use the journal format below to explore different choices you could make regarding how you relate to this area of your life. Take appropriate action and note the results.

JOURNAL WRITING
A. Describe the situation.
B. What is your usual response?
C. What alternative choice or choices did you consider?
D. What were the consequences of your new choices compared with the results of your usual responses?
E. What did you learn? What insight did you gain from this exercise?

PARTICIPANTS' COMMENTS

- A middle school teacher spoke of the change that occurred when she viewed a situation differently. "My class never reached 100 percent school uniform compliance because of one particular student. I became upset with him and so did the rest of the class. I calmed down and took this student out of the room and spoke to him about not wearing his uniform. He became upset because his parents did not have the money to purchase a uniform. We spoke to the principal about the situation. We were able to get previously donated uniforms for this student. I had made the mistake of assuming the student did not want to wear his uniform. By taking a different approach, I was able to correct my misconceptions and find a positive solution."

- Another participant shared, "When my friend died, I created a lot of problems for myself. I blamed his death for my misery and drastic personality and lifestyle changes. Now I realize that it wasn't really his death that caused this – rather, it was how I chose to deal with the loss. If I would have accepted help from those who really cared about me instead of pushing people away and fooling myself into thinking that my actions were really helping my situation, I probably could have avoided wasting so much time hurting myself."

- A man who was participating in my course for drug counselors related an interesting story that is relevant to this particular homework assignment. This was his reason for devoting his life to working with drug addicts: "I was a drug addict who had the experience of kicking the habit. Secondly, because of my addiction, I was a waste to society. Becoming a counselor is a way to pay back my debt to society." His tone conveyed that becoming a drug counselor was his punishment for being a drug addict.

  Another drug counselor who had also been a drug addict responded, "Because I was an addict myself, I look at this job as a drug counselor as a gift from God. To be able to now help others is a blessing."

Two drug counselors relating in very different ways to the same issue of being ex-addicts and counselors.

- Her mother was very upset because her 12 year-old daughter, who used to hold her mother's hand in public, would no longer spend time with her outside their home. "It's not a warm feeling to know that the child you have nurtured since birth is embarrassed to be seen with you."

   I explained that this is a stage of independence that most adolescents go through. Many early adolescents don't want their parents within ten blocks of them when their friends are around. As a result of our discussion, she saw that there were responses to her daughter's behavior other than feeling hurt, resentful and unappreciated. She had more empathy for her daughter when she realized that her daughter was going through a developmental stage that she did not have to take personally.

5

ACCEPTANCE

Profound changes occur when we practice acceptance of ourselves, others and the world we live in.

We have spent the first four chapters of this book discussing choices and changes we can make in order to create more fulfilling lives for ourselves and those we care about. But a necessary step in order for change to occur, is to observe, acknowledge and accept our reality in the present moment. Most of our suffering is a direct result of the programming inside of us that places demands on the world. In other words, **we suffer because we expect circumstances, ourselves and other people to be different from the way they are. In order for change to occur, we must first move from viewing reality as we think it should be to accepting the way it really is.** I'd like to share with you an instance from my own life that exemplifies this point.

My mother is 86 years old, widowed and lives in Florida. In one year she moved out of three different residences. Each time her complaint was that the people were too old, too debilitated or not sophisticated enough. I have actually heard her say as others whizzed by while she crept along with assistance from a walker, "There is no way I can stay here. These people are so old and feeble." For years I angrily tried to tell her that her negative perceptions of others were a reflection of her unhappiness. She wouldn't hear it. After repeated moves, I realized she never grasped the meaning of the saying, "Wherever you go, there you are." She seemed to forget that wherever she went, she took herself (and her problems and perceptions) along with her.

One day I realized that my mother's pattern would always be exactly

61

the same – she would behave the same way when she woke up tomorrow and the day after that. The chance of her changing was practically zero. I acknowledged that instead of fighting and judging her I could choose to accept that this is the way she is and that she most likely would never change. This realization was a turning point for me. My relationship with her dramatically improved when I moved from judgment and resentment to acceptance and empathy.

Another instance of accepting people the way they are rather than how we think they should be was exemplified by a student who spoke about her absent father: "My father is a deadbeat liar. But I feel that I am on my way to accepting him for what he is. Before this class, I had certain expectations of who my father was supposed to be. It would have been nice if he was the person I wanted him to be. Now I accept who he is and doubt if anybody will fulfill all of my expectations."

Accepting that someone is the way they are does not mean that we like or approve of particular aspects of their personality. Acceptance means allowing a person to be the way they are without expecting them to be different.

THE WORD "SHOULD" IS NO GOOD

The story a friend shared with me about his experience of driving to and from the beach each weekend illustrates the power acceptance has to transform our lives.

Tom would leave the city early Friday afternoon in order to avoid the weekend traffic and would return with all the other weekenders on Sunday night. The trip that took two hours going would usually take five coming back. His pattern for years was to sit in his car and get really upset. One Sunday, while inching along in his habitually angry state, he noticed that the driver of the car next to his was joyously singing along with the music from his car radio. It finally hit him, "Both of us are going to get home at the same time but he's having a good time and I'm suffering." From that moment on, his trip back to the city became a totally different experience. The only thing that had changed was his attitude.

He couldn't control the traffic but he could stop demanding that it be different from the way it was.

If we reflect on the previous examples we can see that my mother, the student's father and the traffic are the way they are and probably will not be any different tomorrow. The same observation applies to most people and events in our lives. **We have a choice of accepting people and occurrences the way they are or fighting reality by saying that they "should" be different. The consequence of the first choice is freedom, peace and compassion; whereas the second choice produces conflict, unhappiness and negativity.**

WHO'S THIS STRANGER LIVING IN MY HOUSE?

Let's look at how the "shoulds" negatively influence the harmony and compassion we share with our teenagers. Adolescence is a time for freedom and individual expression. It's a developmental stage similar to walking at one and talking at two. At the same time they're craving independence, teenagers still have to rely on their parents for shelter, food, clothing and money. Behavior such as wearing pants around the knees or painting their nails black are often the only ways for many of them to express their individuality and freedom in an environment where they really have very little power. I encourage you to be tolerant and accept their mode of expression for what it is. By not taking their expression so personally, you can avoid difficult and unnecessary power struggles. This does not imply that anything goes – children need boundaries. There is also no compromising when a child's health, safety and well being are threatened. However, a little tolerance when a teen is testing his or her independence with what are really harmless forms of expression can go a long way toward promoting peace and minimizing more extreme forms of rebellion.

We undermine our relationship with our young children when we think they "should" do something other than express their feelings. Many of us have grown up in the American culture of "doing". We place a great deal of emphasis on how well we "do" anything. We often approach emotions in the same way. When our child is sad, frustrated, angry or impatient we try to "do" something in order to "fix" the situation and make it better. In reality, we must "do" something because we can't bear to just stand by and let our children go through the experience of "feeling". Allowing them to experience their emotions can make us feel inadequate, guilty, helpless and out of control. Underlying this need to "fix" our children is our desire to stop their annoying or painful (to us) emotions so **we can feel better about ourselves.**

We react this way because most of us learned at an early age that certain emotions are not acceptable. For instance crying, sadness or whining could not be tolerated but had to be "fixed". As a result of generations of parents reacting to emotions in this manner we have become a society that can't accept feelings. **It has become the cultural norm to use drugs, alcohol, food and cigarettes to dull, dilute and annihilate feelings.**

A more beneficial approach would be to accept our own as well as our child's feelings. Loving acceptance of our child's (as well as our own) anger, frustration, impatience and whining is probably the most challenging path we can choose. There are many paths to choose from, but in my experience, acceptance is a more compassionate and rewarding choice than denying or "fixing" emotions that we have labeled as negative.

I'M LOOKING AT THE MAN IN THE MIRROR EXERCISE

Often those traits that we have trouble accepting in others are the same ones that we judge as negative in ourselves. As you do the following exercise, you may find that the specific emotions that you don't tolerate in your children are the same ones that you don't accept in yourself. These may also be the same emotions that you were forbidden to express as a child.

1. WHICH OF YOUR CHILD'S EMOTIONAL EXPRESSIONS ARE DIFFICULT FOR YOU TO ACCEPT? (examples: anger, whining, impatience, frustration, loudness, neediness, crying, etc.)

2. WHICH OF YOUR OWN FEELINGS DO YOU HAVE A PROBLEM ACCEPTING?

3. WHEN YOU WERE A CHILD, WHICH FEELINGS WERE YOU NOT ALLOWED TO EXPRESS?

Chastising others for behavior that we judge as negative about ourselves has become one of our favorite pastimes. The critic inside of us who judges the manners, appearance, level of integrity and kindness of others is the same one who gives us a hard time for being ill-mannered, dishonest and not caring enough. I have been biased against people who are overweight. It is no coincidence that I was teased and that I hated myself for being severely overweight between the ages of eight and twelve. I have very little tolerance for people who smoke cigarettes. Again, I was very hard on myself for two years before I finally stopped smoking.

For many of us, this internal judge and jury goes on non-stop day in and day out. It's no wonder that we get upset, feel alienated and run out of energy. Our life dramatically changes in those moments when we suspend this internal negative dialogue and instead accept people, ourselves and reality the way it is.

"I FIND IT EASY TO ACCEPT OTHERS BUT WHEN IT COMES TO ACCEPTING MYSELF, IT'S A WHOLE OTHER STORY"

Many of us have no problem accepting others but when it comes to accepting ourselves it's another story. A colleague of mine once used the analogy of the immune system in discussing the process of self-acceptance. The immune system identifies cells as either "self" or "non self". Once it recognizes a cell as "non self," it targets it for destruction. In the same way, every time we have a thought or emotion that we do not accept, the mind in essence is categorizing it as "non self." In doing this, it is attempting to destroy a part of us that is indeed "self". As we noted in the first chapter, this destructive thought pattern is a major cause of dysfunction or disease. This process applies to anger, lust, jealousy and all the other emotions and thoughts we tend to judge as negative and don't accept as parts of who we are.

I once dated a woman for several months before she told me that she smoked. She said that she hated this part of herself and that she was always afraid that someone would reject her when they found out she smoked. I inquired, "Do you judge yourself negatively while you are smoking a cigarette?" "Yes," she replied. I said, "I think it's a wiser choice to enjoy every puff of that cigarette as long as you are going to smoke." My belief is that non-acceptance and guilt may be as injurious to your health as the cigarette itself.

Along the same lines a teacher reported, "Like a chameleon, I was constantly changing in order to fit in and please those around me. However, once I got in touch with my true self I was able to finally love who God loved, and see who God saw. I saw myself as imperfect and human, as I was intended to be. As a result of this revelation I am now able to forgive and accept others in their humanity on a daily basis."

Some people believe that they must be hard on themselves in order to grow, or that acceptance and change are mutually exclusive. Question number 6 in the Home Assignment asks you to address the acceptance issue in a very profound way by observing the part of you that is hard on yourself. **Accepting who we are in each moment does not mean that we will never change. On the contrary, it is the first step necessary for real change to occur.**

66

ACCEPTANCE

1. WHICH OF YOUR MOTHER'S SPECIFIC BEHAVIOR AND PERSON-
   ALITY TRAITS COULD YOU ACCEPT (EVEN IF SHE HAS PASSED
   AWAY) IN ORDER TO IMPROVE YOUR RELATIONSHIP WITH
   HER AND MAKE YOUR LIFE MORE ENJOYABLE?

2. WHICH OF YOUR FATHER'S SPECIFIC BEHAVIOR AND PERSON-
   ALITY TRAITS COULD YOU ACCEPT (EVEN IF HE HAS PASSED   67
   AWAY) IN ORDER TO IMPROVE YOUR RELATIONSHIP WITH HIM
   AND MAKE YOUR LIFE MORE ENJOYABLE?

3. WHICH OF YOUR CHILDREN'S SPECIFIC BEHAVIOR AND PER-
   SONALITY TRAITS COULD YOU ACCEPT IN ORDER TO IMPROVE
   YOUR RELATIONSHIP WITH THEM AND MAKE YOUR LIFE
   MORE ENJOYABLE?

4. WHICH OF YOUR SIGNIFICANT OTHER'S BEHAVIOR AND PER-SONALITY TRAITS COULD YOU ACCEPT IN ORDER TO IMPROVE YOUR RELATIONSHIP AND MAKE YOUR LIFE MORE ENJOY-ABLE?

5. WHICH SPECIFIC BEHAVIOR AND PERSONALITY TRAITS OF YOUR OWN COULD YOU ACCEPT INSTEAD OF JUDGING AS NEGATIVE?

68

6. FOR ONE HOUR EACH DAY, TRY TO ACCEPT YOUR EVERY THOUGHT, EMOTION AND ACTION. FIRST OBSERVE, THEN DISMISS THE PART OF YOU THAT NEGATIVELY JUDGES YOUR THOUGHTS, ACTIONS AND EMOTIONS.

THE SERENITY PRAYER

"God grant me the serenity to accept the things I cannot change,
the courage to change the things I can,
and the wisdom to know the difference."

PARTICIPANTS' COMMENTS

Strong emotions surface whenever we work on resolving issues with people who are very close to us — especially our parents. Be kind to yourself and your parents.

- A parent responded, "One of the things I have had to accept in my 20-year relationship with my husband is that because I am ready to discuss something, even if I think it is important, doesn't mean that he is ready to hear it."

- A teacher shared, "It used to bother me that my pre-K parents look for any excuse to avoid going on trips or attending parent-teacher conferences. I have begun to understand that I will not get as upset if I accept them as they are. If I force them to do things just to please me, none of us will be satisfied. When I accept them and the situation I feel much better."

- Another teacher commented, "I need to accept the fact that my students, as second language learners, are faced with some unique challenges that directly affect their academic progress. Because their parents cannot help with homework, these students are at a disadvantage. My students are required to work much harder than many public school children do elsewhere because they need to look outside the home for help with their schoolwork...I need to stop being angry at the world for the plight of the students I teach. In order to be more proactive, I need to put that energy into finding alternatives to help students achieve both in and out of school. I also need to accept that I can only do so much to help the 32 children in my class and that sometimes all that I do will just not be enough to promote change."

- A teacher who had recently come from the South shared her feelings of disillusionment about how incredibly different students were in the North compared to the South: "I can't believe the level of disrespect. Children never would think of talking to teachers in the manner that kids do up here. I can't stand being here."

It was obvious that her frustration and pain were mostly caused by her comparison of students from two different locations. She had a big "should" regarding how students were supposed to be. It became clear to her that her way of looking at the issue was not working and that it would be a better choice to start from the point of accepting that these were the students that she was dealing with now, and that they were indeed different from the students that she taught in the South.

- A parent developed a pattern with her sick, cancer-ridden mother. She would tell her about alternative therapies and condemn her for not wanting to try them. This approach consistently created arguments and stress. As part of her acceptance homework she wrote: "I finally realized that our conflict was rooted in my inability to accept that my mother did not believe in alternative therapies. Instead of giving her advice, I told my mother how much I loved and cared for her. This dramatically changed our level of interaction." (Sounds like a great alternative therapy to me!)

- After doing this homework, a woman shared, "I am 32 years old and my mother lives with me. If I'm wearing a dress that is in the least bit revealing when I leave the house, I have to put a sweater over it or my mother will get upset."

"Is there any chance your mother will change?" I asked her.

"No," she replied, "I've tried to talk to her and remind her that I'm 32 years old and it is my house she is living in. This discussion never did any good. Now I just accept that this is the way she is and I take my sweater off as soon as I get outside."

(*Note:* This is the same strategy that teenagers often use with their parents.)

- A teacher told us that before understanding the principle of acceptance, she constantly put herself down for working and not spending enough time with her daughter. In her homework she responded, "I used to be real hard on myself for not spending enough time with my daughter. I have to accept the fact that it is a necessity for me to work and the consequence is that I cannot spend as much time as I would like with my daughter. When I accept this reality and don't judge myself as a bad mother, my daughter seems to be more understanding."

- When asked, "What do you need to accept about your father?" one woman said, "I used to idolize my father and look at him as if he had no faults at all. No man could ever live up to my expectations and as a result, I have yet to have a successful relationship with a man. I now see this pattern clearly. I am also seeing that my father does have faults and that he is a human being like everyone else. This has allowed me to be more realistic in my expectations of men."

71

- A parent complained that her mother gives card parties at her house several times a week and cooks for everyone. She felt her mother was being taken advantage of because no one else offered to prepare any food. "Do you think your mother enjoys cooking for these people?" I asked her. "Yes," she responded. "Well, you might want to accept the fact that giving to others makes your mother happy."

- A mother stated, "I find myself being disappointed by people all the time. My husband is always late, but every time he tells me he'll meet me somewhere at a certain time, I always believe him. My boss at work has lied to me several times, yet whenever she tells me something I always believe her and inevitably I am disappointed."

  Her suffering was the result of viewing people from the vantage point of how she wanted them to be rather than how they really were. She was unwilling to accept the fact that people don't always tell the truth.

- In an ongoing personal growth course I recently attended, Robert stood up and shared how he became upset every time Anthony spoke. He said that he found Anthony to be inauthentic in his expression and he cringed each time Anthony opened his mouth. This was very interesting because each time Robert spoke he was unable to be "real" in his expression. It was obvious to me that Robert was negatively judging Anthony for the same characteristics he possessed.

- A teacher wrote about her experience, "Prior to enrolling in this course, I was of the opinion that acceptance meant agreement. It was quite a revelation to learn that acceptance of a person's negative behavior is a mere acknowledgment of who the individual is, but not necessarily a condoning of those traits. I eventually accepted the fact that a particularly difficult student of mine was a troubled child with very little or no structure. By accepting him I was better able to discipline him in a sincere, loving manner."

- A teacher's response clearly exemplified the intention of question 6:

    "I found myself wanting to avoid the assignment because I had no desire to feel anything negative or to feel good about negative thoughts. I began to realize that the thought was not necessarily what caused the discomfort. It was the negative judgment that I had about the thought that made me feel uneasy. I realized that I am very judgmental of myself and that little room is allowed for error. Whenever an error is made I beat myself up before anyone else can.

    After allowing myself to go through the process several times, one question came to mind, 'How real am I if I only allow myself to look at and accept nice, kind, gentle, sweet thoughts but do not allow myself to look at and see that there are things about me that I may not be totally content with?' I realized that I am no less a person if I do not react to a situation the way I felt I should have."

6

RESPONSIBILITY
WHO IS CONTROLLING YOUR LIFE?

Being responsible begins with viewing each situation from the perspective of how we created, promoted or allowed what is present.

We live in a society that often seems to reward a victim mentality. On daytime talk shows I often observe someone ranting about how they were "done in" by someone else. Although I have empathy, I still want to ask, "What part did you play? How did you create, promote or allow this to happen?" This is what we mean by taking responsibility for what happens in our lives.

Ask yourself this question: "When was I a victim?" Tell about a time when you were picked on, treated unfairly or blamed for something that wasn't your fault. A ninth grade student's recent response was an attempt to justify her victimization: "This girl was mad at some of us and we were just standing there when she hit me. I didn't say anything to her."

"Had you spoken negatively about her behind her back?" I asked. In answering "yes", she saw how subtle and profound taking responsibility could be. **Taking responsibility is not about being right or wrong. It's about looking at what part we play in creating, promoting or allowing what happens in our lives.**

A single mother spoke angrily about the "dog" that left her.

I asked her, "Who chose that dog?"

If we choose to point blame and dwell in victimization, what we get is anger, hurt and no resolution. **We become powerful, effective and fulfilled when we see ourselves as the cause of what our lives look like in any particular moment.**

A mother at first spoke of how her "mean" husband was always putting her down and didn't allow her to give her opinion on most issues. As the classes progressed, she began looking at the part she played in the situation. She realized that she "promoted" this situation by not being assertive and by letting him get away with this behavior. Eventually she started telling him how his comments made her feel and that she wasn't going to put up with it. For many years she "allowed" him to talk to her in a hurtful manner. She took responsibility for changing the pattern by speaking up.

In another instance, a woman was speaking sadly about the fact that in her culture it was basically acceptable for married men to have other lovers. I inquired, "Is this type of behavior okay with you?" She responded that she was very hurt by her husband seeing other women. I asked her how she created, promoted or allowed this type of behavior. She acknowledged promoting it by not speaking up and saying how it hurt her. The next session she reported that she had told her husband how hurt she was. He denied any wrongdoing but they both knew the truth. She demanded that he be faithful. Over the next month she reported that he wasn't cheating and he treated her with a lot more respect – basically, the respect that she now demanded.

One of my high school students summed up this lesson on her final exam when she wrote, "I realized I have a part in how my relationship with anyone looks. Rather than blaming others, I now look inside myself to see how I have created what is present. If I do this, I am in control of my life. **If I blame others, they are controlling me.**"

YOU ARE THE ENVIRONMENT YOUR CHILDREN GROW UP IN

What we are communicating to our children in each moment is how we are feeling. Masterful Parenting is about becoming aware of and taking responsibility for this internal environment. In every moment, these emotions are creating the environment our children grow up in. Young children are very sensitive – they are like sponges absorbing and then reacting to everything in their environment. Researchers have observed what has been termed the "switching phenomenon." When we are under stress, the electrical polarity of our body is "switched". When an infant is in contact with parents who are constantly stressed, or when a mother is under stress while her child is in utero, the child's electrical polarity is also constantly being switched. Children, especially infants, are very susceptible to being weakened because they don't have the capacity to filter out what is negative from what is positive. This electrical imbalance or reversed polarity is repeatedly noted in people with chronic fatigue, depression, cancer, autoimmune diseases and ADHD.

When we think negative thoughts and feel anger, our children are living in an angry environment. When we view our children critically through the eyes of judgment, they are being raised in an unsafe environment. When we constantly worry, our children are being brought up in a fearful environment. Children who speak disrespectfully to their parents are usually being raised in a home where parents speak disrespectfully to their children and/or to each other and where the parents don't demonstrate the resolve to speak up and not tolerate their child's disrespectful tone of voice.

The emotional quality of our home environment is not only affected by our attitude toward our children at any particular moment, but also by how we relate to other family members. It's like second-hand smoke – we are polluting our environment when we are constantly angry with our spouse or other inhabitants of our home. Children will grow strong in a nurturing environment – one that provides caring, understanding and loving attention. It's like a rose bush that responds to watering, care and an understanding of its growth cycle.

Along with the emotional environment, the physical and intellectual environment that we create for our children also has a tremendous effect on their well being. Everyone feels calmer and more centered in a home that is neat, clean and organized. When we create a space to go to that is private and quiet, we create an atmosphere that is beneficial for good study habits.

Studies related to how television affects our intellectual environment have shown that the brain can function on two very distinct levels: a "responding level" and a "thinking level." The rapid stimulation of TV locks the brain into "responding" mode, which eliminates the possibility of reflection, analytical thought, intellectual challenge and sustained or focused attention. As time in front of the television increases (the average American viewer spends 28 hours a week watching TV), viewers experience a shorter attention span, an impaired capacity to stick with a problem, reduced comprehension of complexities in language, and diminished listening ability. Video games have a similar effect. The responsibility lies with the parents to determine how many hours a day their children watch television and play video games.

As parents of school children, we are not the only influence in our children's lives, but children raised in a home environment of love, caring and empathy have very different beliefs about who they are compared to children raised in an environment permeated with anger, tension, judgment and fear.

LIFE IS EASY WHEN IT'S EASY, BUT...

You've had a brutal day at work, it's 95 degrees, the humidity is 95 percent, and you've spent the last 45 minutes on a crowded bus without air conditioning. You're already in a bad mood as you walk into your house and observe your 16-year-old daughter on the phone, oblivious to the music blasting in the living room. Think about the thoughts and emotions you would have, given your existing mood. Not pretty, I bet. Now imagine walking into the same situation after just being told you received an unexpected pay raise at work and your best friend gave you a ride home in her beautiful new air conditioned car. Your thoughts, emotional state and reaction to your daughter and her music would most likely be quite different.

We are responsible for our moods and the consequences of the actions we take depending on our moods. Moods don't come from the outside. Rather, they most often develop from choices in thinking that we make regarding the events in our lives.

For example, earlier today I went out to mail a package. After driving the two-mile dirt road that leads from my house to the main road, I realized that I had forgotten a book that I wanted to include in the package. I raced home (the post office was closing soon) only to discover that I had never brought the book to my house in the first place. I then raced back to the post office and mailed the package. Returning to my car I heard a hissing sound being made by air escaping where a sharp rock had punctured my tire. The air was leaking slowly. I got into my car and started driving to the repair shop. On the way there, I got behind a school bus. A trip that should have taken three minutes instead took ten. The mechanic was able to patch the tire but said I would need a new one because all the air had leaked out and the sidewall had collapsed and been damaged. I drove to the tire store to find out that they no longer had my size tire. The story doesn't end here, but I'll stop.

Now, was it the tire's fault that I was in a bad mood? Did the school bus cause my emotional state? Or was it thoughts like, "I have no luck", "God is punishing me" and "Life sucks" that caused me to be emotionally upset? I think you'll agree that I chose the negative thoughts which, in turn, produced my bad mood. In fact, for about thirty seconds I indulged in these negative thoughts and emotions, but I soon snapped out of it and began to laugh.

The challenge always occurs when things get tough. The most important thing to do when we're in a bad mood is to observe and notice that we are in a bad mood. Knowing this gives us the choice to react from this place or to take a "time out" and relax before we proceed. A short time out isn't always enough to change our mood. Sometimes we need to read a book, exercise, listen to calming music, take a warm bath, or walk around the block in order to re-establish some semblance of peace inside of ourselves. How we relate to any issue determines whether we're going to create a bad mood or a good mood. As always, the choice is ours.

RESPONSIBILITY

1. WRITE DOWN AT LEAST ONE SITUATION WHERE YOU FELT
    PICKED ON, TREATED UNFAIRLY OR BLAMED FOR SOMETHING
    THAT YOU FELT WASN'T YOUR FAULT. WRITE THE SITUATION
    DOWN AS IF YOU WERE A VICTIM.

78

2. WRITE ABOUT THE SAME SITUATION FROM THE VIEWPOINT
    WHERE YOU CREATED, PROMOTED OR ALLOWED THE
    SITUATION TO HAPPEN. ALSO, LOOK AT THE CHOICES YOU
    MADE IN YOUR REACTION TO THE SITUATION. WRITE DOWN
    POSSIBLE CHOICES THAT YOU COULD HAVE MADE THAT MAY
    HAVE BEEN MORE BENEFICIAL TO YOURSELF AND OTHERS.

PARTICIPANTS' COMMENTS

- A mother was really upset. Her son came home with terrible grades in three out of five junior high school classes. He said it wasn't his fault; the teachers just didn't like him. He had an excuse for every poor grade. The mother explained that in the past, when her son had problems with teachers in school, she would go and find out why the teachers were picking on him. It became obvious to her and everyone else in the class how she promoted her son's victim consciousness by supporting him when he blamed his teachers for his poor grades.

- A middle school dean reported his experience of teaching a course after a five-year absence from the classroom. "That first class was horrible. After ten minutes there was no discipline – the kids were all over the place. That night I was really angry. I blamed the school, the parents and the 'youth of today' for the unruly behavior.

  "After our class on responsibility, I considered that I may have something to do with my students' disrespect. When I did this, I realized that not having prepared a lesson plan for the first class may have contributed to the chaos in the room. The next time I met with my students I spent a considerable amount of time preparing for the class. The tone and the behavior of the students were totally transformed."

- A woman said that her husband was told to stop smoking by his doctor because he had pre-malignant cells present after a biopsy. He continued to smoke, which upset her a great deal. I asked her how old he was. She said that he was 52. Although it was difficult to do, she needed to see her husband as responsible for his own actions.

- Several years ago I was thinking about starting a school based on the principles that I now teach in my classes. I spent a considerable amount of time traveling to schools around the country in order to observe teachers who were exemplary in what they taught. When I

79

went to a Middle School in South Central Los Angeles I was told by the administrators and other teachers to observe a certain math teacher. When I sat in his class I was impressed by the total absorption of the students. After class I asked him why he was such a successful teacher.

He responded, "The average student who enters the seventh grade at this school has achieved a third grade math level. I know that each and every student is capable of achieving a ninth grade math level by the time they complete the ninth grade. More often than not these students achieve that level of expectation. I have taken time to develop interesting and motivating lesson plans that incorporate hands on experimentation. I have also taken the responsibility of extending myself to my students by providing my home telephone number in order to address any problems or difficulties they may be facing."

7

FORGIVENESS

Forgiveness is one of the greatest gifts we can give to ourselves.

A father's lengthy and angry response when asked, "Who do you need to forgive?" can provide us with a good starting point for the exploration of this very important principle.

"I will never forgive my brother-in-law. We had a fight just before he married my sister. He thought that I felt that he was not good enough for her. Words led to threats, threats became blows and it ended up in an all out fight. Although I see him at family functions at least twice a year, I haven't spoken to him since the incident occurred more than twelve years ago."

After further discussion, this father revealed that he felt sad whenever he saw his brother-in-law and that it had definitely had a negative effect on his relationship with his sister, with whom he had previously been very close. He now realized that he was demonstrating a "revenge" or "eye for an eye" response. I pointed out that there are perceived benefits to every choice we make. Some potential advantages to responding in a vengeful manner might include:

- Blaming others

- Not taking responsibility for our part in what happened in the situation

- Proclaiming and defending our innocence... Everyone else is guilty

- Being right... It's the others who are wrong

- Believing that the world is unfair and people are hurt without reason

- Justifying our bitterness, anger and rage

- Not having to examine the part we played in the situation

- Feeling betrayed

The problem with all of these so called "benefits" is that they result in decreased love and vitality. In the same situation, forgiveness is an alternate response that we can choose, which offers these potential outcomes:

- Taking responsibility for our part in the situation

- Choosing to let go of feeling betrayed

- Beginning to heal our hurt and experiencing increased vitality

- Being aware that harmony is more important than being right and declaring the other person wrong

- Learning through compassion the lessons that the situation has to teach us rather than justifying our anger and rage

When we stop blaming others and take responsibility, we experience the increased vitality and love that healing brings. In contrast, revenge keeps us living in the past, attached to our hatred and unable to heal. **We hurt ourselves deeply in order to justify hurting someone else and being right.**

By not forgiving we can expect:	*By forgiving we can expect:*
1. *Getting to be right by blaming others*	1. *Inner peace, empathy, love and vitality*
2. *Experiencing bitterness and rage*	2. *Learning from our experiences*
3. *Feeling betrayal and inner pain*	3. *Healing and the acceptance of what is*

There are several common misconceptions regarding the act of forgiveness. Many people believe that the other person must apologize first before forgiveness can ever be considered. This is a false premise. Not only does the other person not have to apologize first, he doesn't even have to be alive in order for forgiveness to occur. Forgiveness doesn't depend at all on the person or persons being forgiven. **Forgiveness is an internal process that makes the necessary room in the heart for empathy.**

Many people view forgiveness as something nice we do for someone else (who doesn't deserve it in the first place). In reality, when we forgive we release the negativity we are feeling for the other person. We let go of them. Without forgiveness we continue to carry the people we have not forgiven around with us. Scientists have observed an elevated heart rate and higher blood pressure in people who are trapped in their negativity. On the other hand, when we forgive, we experience internal calm and a healing of the part of ourselves that has been hurt. **More than an act of kindness to another, forgiveness is an act of kindness to ourselves.**

83

Another misconception is the belief that when we forgive someone, we are condoning his or her behavior. There is always the choice to forgive and at the same time make it clear that we do not appreciate the behavior. In fact, we can forgive and choose not to interact with that person anymore.

Often we are disappointed when feelings of anger and hatred reappear upon seeing, hearing or thinking about a person or situation. **Forgiveness is usually not a one-time event but an ongoing process that often requires the experiencing and acceptance of a great deal of anger.**

I WAS BETRAYED

Betrayal is a key issue in many situations that provoke anger, retaliation and non-forgiveness. **We take other people's behavior personally and call it betrayal when, in fact, they are really just doing what they have always**

done. If we observe closely, we will probably see that the person who is habitually breaking his agreements with us, has most likely done the same to others. When we realize this fact, we have the choice to judge them for their behavior or to simply accept them for who they are. Again, it's always our choice.

SELF-FORGIVENESS

For many of us, forgiving ourselves can be even more challenging than forgiving others. Ask yourself, "What haven't I forgiven myself for?" For example, a very caring parent said she had a hard time forgiving herself for yelling at her child. She was hard on herself and judged herself as abusive and inconsiderate. On one level, she could have forgiven herself for her actions. On a deeper level, she needed to forgive herself for judging herself so harshly. Think about it. Being inconsiderate or abusive is not who we are. They are two behaviors among many that we are capable of manifesting. We need to realize that at any particular moment, we are all capable of any type of behavior. Destructive behavior and mistakes can be viewed as an opportunity to learn and grow or as an opportunity to beat ourselves up…. As always, the choice is ours.

84

FORGIVENESS EXERCISE

You Are Always Hurt by the One You Love

1. AT THE TOP OF A PIECE OF PAPER, WRITE THE NAME OF SOMEONE WITH WHOM YOU WERE CLOSE BUT WITH WHOM, BECAUSE OF TENSION, YOU NO LONGER COMMUNICATE. THIS PERSON COULD BE A RELATIVE, EX-LOVER, EX-SPOUSE, EX-FRIEND, ETC. ONE OF THOSE "EXES".

2. UNDER THIS PERSON'S NAME, MAKE TWO SEPARATE LISTS – ONE FOR GOOD QUALITIES, THE OTHER FOR BAD. CONSIDER STRENGTHS, WEAKNESSES AND QUALITIES, SUCH AS: SENSE OF HUMOR, INTELLIGENCE, INTEGRITY, KINDNESS, EMPATHY, HONESTY, PHYSICAL ATTRACTIVENESS, ETC.

More often that not, that once-close person with whom we now can't communicate is someone who we feel has hurt us and whom we have not forgiven. **It is impossible to communicate openly with someone we have not forgiven.**

Especially when the "Ex" was an intimate relationship, the exercise also helps us acknowledge positive qualities that attracted us in the first place. In most cases, the person who we hate so much is someone we once loved. **The anger that is often felt is not the opposite of love, but actually part of love.** Beneath anger is hurt and lying beneath the hurt is love. Acknowledging both the love and the hurt can create the possibility of forgiveness and the subsequent sense of well being that comes from letting go. I am not saying that everyone can change their attitude from hatred to forgiveness overnight. It can be a long process, often requiring counseling and the processing of a great deal of emotion. What I hope, though, is that this chapter will bring the awareness that forgiveness is always an option and a choice. Lastly, I hope that you are now motivated to forgive, understanding that if you chose to no one will benefits more than you.

FORGIVENESS OF SELF AND OTHERS

1. WHAT HAVE YOU NOT FORGIVEN YOURSELF FOR?

86

2. WHAT HAS SOMEONE ELSE NOT FORGIVEN YOU FOR?

3. WHO HAVEN'T YOU FORGIVEN?

4. WHY DO WE NEED TO FORGIVE?

87

What we get by not forgiving:

- Get to be right
- No responsibility
- Blame
- Justify bitterness and rage
- Justify betrayal
- Inner pain, no healing

What we get by forgiving:

- Inner peace
- Lessons learned
- Take responsibility
- Love and vitality
- No betrayal, just what is
- Healing

PARTICIPANTS' COMMENTS

- When asked, "What have you not forgiven yourself for?" a mother from Nigeria responded that she had received two messages from her uncle in her homeland. She loved this man deeply, but decided to wait until the weekend to call him back because it was much cheaper. When she called back, she was told that he had just passed away. She cried as she told this story and said that even though it had happened three years earlier, she still couldn't forgive herself for not calling back as soon as she had received the messages. She did admit, however, that in the past she had waited for the cheaper weekend rates to return calls, and that the messages had given no indication that her uncle was sick.

  I pointed to another woman in the group and asked the Nigerian woman, "If this woman did exactly what you did, could you forgive her?" She thought about it and realized that she could forgive the other women. I asked, "Can you see the possibility of forgiving yourself?" She reflected and said, "It will be hard, but I can see the possibility."

- A teacher from a foreign country said that although her reaction seemed extreme to many of her colleagues, she could not forgive her husband for smoking. "When I met my husband, he smoked. I hate the smell of smoke. I told him that if he smoked, I would not marry him. He said that he would quit and he did. But last year, I found out that he was smoking behind my back. At first he lied. Then he said that he would never do it again. Several months later, I found out that he was still smoking. I am thinking about getting a divorce because of this."

  A classmate responded, "My sister had the same problem with her husband. What she did was to allow her husband to smoke outside the house but never inside the house. It seems to work for them."

  I asked, "Are you upset because he smokes or because he didn't keep his word?"

  She replied, "I want to divorce him because he betrayed me."

88

I made her aware that the issue was his lying about smoking and not the act of smoking itself. The class also pointed out that she had essentially given him no choice but to lie. She never would have accepted the truth. We also discussed that her rationale for wanting a divorce may have been to get even by punishing her spouse. This is an example of the "eye for an eye" consciousness that we discussed earlier.

After pointing this out, I said, "I know the divorce will most likely hurt your husband deeply but what will you lose by not seeing him anymore?" She became quite sad and shared that she really loved him and that by leaving him she would be losing a great deal. Often, in our anger, we forget that when we take our heart away from another as a way of punishing them, we punish ourselves as well.

- A teacher shared, "I need to deal with my guilt. Because of teaching, I am not able to spend a lot of time with my own young children. This is a very hard thing for me and I try to compensate by doing special things or buying them treats whenever I can. But then I feel guilty for spoiling them."

Another teacher responded that being a teacher was a choice and one of the consequences of that choice was not being able to be a traditional housewife. But a positive consequence of being a teacher was that the lessons learned working with the children in school could make her a better parent to her own children.

- This mother's sharing after doing the forgiveness homework was a profound demonstration of the power of forgiveness.

"I realized for the first time that I looked at my 10-year-old son differently than my daughter. I didn't like what I saw because I saw his father's face who I never forgave for cheating on me. I broke down and cried. I felt so sad for my son and didn't like myself for being so cruel. When I recovered, I saw that I needed to do whatever it took to forgive his father so I could be more loving to my son."

- I would like to share a personal experience. Some time ago, I had an argument with my girlfriend while we were visiting a beautiful foreign city. I just stormed off and we each toured the city alone. I got back to where we were staying six hours after she did because I had missed the train. We didn't speak until the next morning. When I woke up, I apologized and began to cry very deeply. This experience of apologizing was different from any other I had ever had. As I was crying, I was realizing and apologizing for any pain I had caused her or anyone else.

  Since the experience I have become much kinder to her. Not because I feel guilty but because something deep inside of me was released by going to that level. The profound healing I experienced arose from my feeling a deep level of remorse for any suffering I had ever inflicted on anyone, ever. I know it doesn't serve us to beat ourselves up but it does seem that experiencing and expressing our deep remorse can have incredible value. What is your experience?

8

COMMUNICATION
IT AIN'T WHAT YOU SAY...OR IS IT?

The key to having successful relationships is the ability to experience what we are feeling and to communicate that feeling to other people in a respectful manner.

Experts who study communication tell us that there are three primary modes or styles of communication: passive, aggressive and assertive. Take a few minutes to answer the following questions to see how each mode is different, and to determine which style you use most often.

91

WHAT IS YOUR MODE OF COMMUNICATION?

CIRCLE THE RESPONSE THAT IS TRUEST FOR YOU.
Please answer openly and honestly by indicating how you actually are and not how you would like to be or how you would like to be seen.

Always true (at least 90% of the time)
Often true (75% of the time)
Sometimes true (50% of the time)
Rarely true (25% of the time)
Never true (less than 10% of the time)

1.   *I enjoy meeting new people*
     Always   Often   Sometimes   Rarely   Never

2.   *I have a right to say "no" to things I don't want to do*
     Always   Often   Sometimes   Rarely   Never

3. *I have a right to express my feelings*
   Always   Often   Sometimes   Rarely   Never

4. *A person can change how he or she gets along with others*
   Always   Often   Sometimes   Rarely   Never

5. *I have a right to ask for what I need*
   Always   Often   Sometimes   Rarely   Never

6. *It is easy for me to say "no" to things I don't want to do*
   Always   Often   Sometimes   Rarely   Never

7. *I don't let others boss me around*
   Always   Often   Sometimes   Rarely   Never

8. *It is easy for me to express negative feelings like anger*
   Always   Often   Sometimes   Rarely   Never

9. *I have trouble controlling my temper*
   Always   Often   Sometimes   Rarely   Never

10. *I am honest about my feelings with friends*
    Always   Often   Sometimes   Rarely   Never

INTERPRETING THE RESULTS

Let's score your answers to reveal your predominant mode of communication. Then we will define each mode.

SCORING TABLE

Always	5 points
Often	4 points
Sometimes	3 points
Rarely	2 points
Never	1 point

PASSIVITY SCALE

Using the scoring from above, add up your points from questions 1-9. A score of 27 or below indicates a **PASSIVE** communicator.

ASSERTIVENESS SCALE

Using the scoring table above, add up your points from questions 1-7. A score of 28 or above indicates an **ASSERTIVE** communicator.

AGGRESSIVENESS SCALE

Using the scoring table from above, add up your points from questions 7-9. A score of 12 or above indicates an **AGGRESSIVE** communicator.

The purpose of this scoring is not only to learn about your habitual mode of communication, but also to show that people are very different and can vary widely regarding their particular style of expression. If someone is passive, we need to be patient and encourage them to speak their truth. If they are the aggressive type, we need to help them get past their anger in order to communicate more effectively.

THE THREE PRIMARY MODES OF COMMUNICATING
(PASSIVE, AGGRESSIVE, ASSERTIVE)

In observing your mode of communication, you need to take into account that our style of communication often changes depending on who we are speaking to. You may be habitually passive with one person and consistently aggressive with someone else. For instance, you might be habitually aggressive with your mother but fall into a passive habit with your father. The key term here is "habitual pattern". A lot of times the "safe" people get our anger while the ones we fear get our silence. It's fine to choose to be passive sometimes and to choose to be aggressive at other times with a particular person. However, problems arise when we don't choose but, instead, communicate in a habitual pattern that usually does not serve us.

With this is mind, let's take a look at some of the thought patterns that are behind the different styles. Listed below are several "reasons" for being a passive communicator followed by a list of "reasons" for communicating aggressively. Circle any that apply to your interaction with anyone in your life.

Passive communicating means not saying what you think, feel, need or want. When you are passive, you are putting another person's needs before your own because...

1. You are afraid to risk the consequences.

2. You don't want to "make waves".

3. You think it's more important to be liked than to say what you want to say.

4. You don't want to be noticed or call attention to yourself.

5. You are afraid of being wrong.

6. You don't believe in your right to express your wants, needs, feelings and opinions.

7. You think another person's rights are more important than yours.

8.   You think it takes too much energy to say something that probably won't do any good anyway.

9.   You are influenced by your culture.

10. You have allowed it to become a habit.

11. You have been hurt by aggression and do not wish to hurt others.

12. You feel that you will be hurt or taken advantage of if you express your feelings.

Aggressive communicating means saying what you think, feel, want or need without respecting the feelings of others. When you are aggressive, you are putting your own needs before the needs of others because...

1.   You don't want to acknowledge the hurt behind your anger.

2.   You were never taught a different way to communicate.

3.   You don't want people having power or taking advantage of you.

4.   You find it easier to be aggressive.

5.   You have allowed it to become a habit.

6.   You want to control the situation.

7.   You don't like hearing "no".

8.   You can't hold the feeling of anger inside yourself so you release it on others.

ASSERTIVE COMMUNICATION: FINDING THE MIDDLE GROUND

Ideally, passive and aggressive styles can be replaced with assertive communication. Assertive communicating means saying what you think, feel or want in a way that respects your needs as well as the needs of the other person because...

1.   You want to communicate in a way that respects others.

2.   You want to communicate in a straightforward, clear and non-threatening way.

3.   You want to communicate in a way that respects your own rights.

The key to replacing an aggressive style with assertive communication is to communicate the **hurt feeling** rather than the anger. The key to replacing a passive style with assertive communication is to communicate the hurt feeling rather than not saying anything at all. **It requires courage to be vulnerable and speak our truth.** The "ABC" formula provides a practical tool for promoting more peaceful relationships through assertive communication:

A – WHEN YOU SAY OR DO...

B – I "FEEL"...

C – I "NEED"...

This formula, besides promoting your own assertive communication, can be particularly helpful when conflicts arise.

Passive types attempt to resolve conflict by not saying anything. Often these people are not in touch with their needs and feelings in the moment. This lack of awareness usually is the results of internal moral judgments as to which feelings are acceptable and which needs are justifiable. Is it selfish to need respect, love, security, or to be heard? Or maybe, is it our right as human beings to express and fulfill our needs? These are questions that people who are habitually not speaking their truth might want to ask themselves. **Again, the key to having successful relationships is the ability to experience what you are feeling and communicate that feeling to other people in a respectful manner; i.e., assertive communication.** This applies to every relationship in your life, whether it is with your spouse, your children, your friends, your co-worker or anyone we interact with.

When you look more closely at aggressive patterns of communication, you will see that anger is most often our response to a specific hurt, such as feeling disrespected, being taken advantage of, not being heard, feeling betrayed, tense, tired, embarrassed or vulnerable. The anger is always one step removed from the hurt. The way to move from a response of anger to assertive communication is to acknowledge and express the hurt you are feeling, first to yourself and then to the other person. You will experience very different outcomes if you say, "I feel betrayed, disrespected, taken advantage of or hurt" rather than blowing up and yelling. **Assertive communication produces an inner sense of integrity because you are speaking your truth, and at the same time promotes real intimacy because you're being vulnerable.**

I'M NOT SUPPOSED TO GET SO ANGRY AT SOMEONE I LOVE

It's my experience that the people we love the most (family members, friends, significant others) bring out our anger the most. You might think that if you love someone, you're not supposed to get angry at them. But this belief does not withstand the test of reality. Loved ones have the ability to hurt us at the deepest level exactly because we love them so much. **Anger is not the opposite of love. It is a response to the hurt we feel because we love.** Because we are easily hurt by these "special" people, we are often the most vulnerable around them.

It takes a lot of courage to be vulnerable and express our hurt. Kids today spend a lot of energy acting tough, wearing "gangsta" clothes, dressing in black, getting tattoos and having different body parts pierced. But this tough facade is really the opposite of being vulnerable, it's more like a form of fear – the fear of being real and expressing how they really feel. Similarly, the word "whatever" has become a mantra for many youngsters who pretend to be cool and aloof rather than express what is going on inside of them.

When we, as parents, communicate how we feel and what we need in a respectful manner, we're showing our children a better way – a way that promotes loving relationships and success in life.

FEELINGS FOLLOW THOUGHTS...BUT TO FEEL IS REAL

Hurt is what drives anger. An habitual response might be to get angry and to yell at your girlfriend when you see her talking to another guy. The assertive approach would be to tell her that when she flirts with another guy you feel jealous and abandoned.

It gets a little tricky when we realize that behind the hurt is often a negative thought. Some psychologists suggest an alternative approach: looking at the negative thinking that causes the jealousy in the first place. A belief such as, "If she talks to another guy, it means that she is going to leave me," might be generating the hurt and anger. When we realize this, we might be able to better understand the situation, calm our emotions, and not even have to communicate our jealousy. This way of viewing situations makes us responsible for our behavior rather then blaming others for our emotional state.

I have friends who are able to go to this level of understanding in many situations that have the potential for emotional upheaval. In most cases, these individuals have been working on themselves for a long time and have developed a deep understanding of their own as well as others' emotional nature. But for one friend in particular, it is easy for him to control his emotions because he is not in touch with how he feels. This is an example of behavior on the outside being generated by very different reasons on the inside. This form of non-vulnerability is very common in a society such as ours which prizes emotional control over emotional expression. We must be cautious when observing ourselves and others to see what is motivating behavior. Is it a suppressed fear of emotions or an advanced emotional understanding?

A vast majority of the parents who participate in the Masterful Parenting program are neither emotional masters nor control freaks. Rather, they are stuck in an aggressive or passive pattern of expression that produces a great deal of stress for themselves and their families. The challenge for many is first to recognize their habitual style of communication and then to observe their feelings and communicate them in an assertive manner. This is very difficult to do, **but when an unconscious negative pattern of behavior is broken and a different choice is made, we feel a joy inside that comes from knowing we have done the right thing.**

FEED THE NEED

Along with feelings, we all have needs that must be internally acknowledged and communicated. Needs such as food, shelter and to be loved are common to all of us. The need to contribute to our own well-being and the well being of others, although extremely profound, is often not acknowledged. From an early age, girls are taught that their needs aren't that important, and that what is important is caring for and nurturing others. Boys are taught that in order to be strong they should endure hardship without showing pain and that they shouldn't have to rely on others for support. I have observed how differently boys and girls relate to someone who has been hurt during a sports activity. Girls will run over to an injured girl and try to help her whereas the boys will usually ignore a boy who is laying on the ground, expecting him to be "tough enough" to make it off the playing field on his own.

Along with recognizing and communicating our needs, it is also essential to understand the specific needs of others. Instead of recognizing our children's needs, we often manipulate them by using guilt, fear, reward, punishment, shame and obligation. Manipulation based communication might work in the moment to get them to do what we want but in the long run it does not create an environment of trust, nor does it foster open relationships. For instance, a mother could tell her 14 year-old daughter that if she doesn't clean the dishes she will not be able to go to her best friend's birthday party.

Alternately the mother could balance her need to have support around the house with her daughter's desire to contribute out of a need to be treated as an integral part of the family. When this happens an environment is created of sharing and helping each other as part of a cohesive family. After years of functioning in such an environment of trust, mutual respect and cooperation, the mother's communication might be, "I need your help with the dishes. I know you need to go to your friend's party. How can we make this work for both of us?" Creating a loving, respectful environment fulfills a very deep need in every family member. Isn't that what we all wanted and needed as children?

HABIT VS. CONSCIOUS CHOICE

We can't possibly be effective in our lives if we fail to express our inner truth in a way that respects others. For this to happen, we must first become aware of what mode of communication we use. We need to observe the habitual roles we play and consciously make new, more beneficial choices. As we get better at this, we can decide the outcome we want beforehand and communicate in a way that will achieve the desired result.

100

This was exemplified by Lewis, a participant in one of my parenting classes. Lewis had a job in a warehouse where he was responsible for distributing and keeping track of expensive diagnostic equipment. The workers would sign the equipment out for a five-day period but they almost never returned it on time. Lewis would have to hunt them down and nag them which made him very upset. So much so, that when he saw the workers hanging out in the parking lot before work, he would get really angry.

After the class on communication, Lewis became more aware of his habitually angry response. He saw that all of his anger was getting him nowhere. He became more accepting and was able to joke with the other workers. When they explained why they usually returned the equipment late, he was able to empathize. He told me, "Work became more enjoyable. You wouldn't believe it but the more calmly I asked them why the equipment was late instead of getting angry, the more often the equipment got back on time."

A mother from one of my classes shared how changing her usual mode of communication helped smooth things over with her daughter. "I observed that sometimes my pattern of communication with my daughter was too aggressive," she said. "When I saw that chores weren't done or homework was started late, I would lose my temper. I often began my communication with, 'Didn't I tell you to do this?' or 'Why isn't this done yet?' or 'Why are you still sitting here?' Things would go downhill from there. She would get angry or I would get angry and nothing would be gained. When I began to approach my daughter differently by explaining her responsibilities and telling her how I felt when she was not honoring her agreement, things began to change." **It is not easy to change habitual patterns, and being gentle with yourself is very important, especially at times when you think you have "blown it".**

Another student shared that all he had to do to win an argument with his girlfriend was to tell her to "get out" and she would give in. His aggressiveness forced her to be passive. This is an example of manipulation, not open communication. If we care about a person, are we really serving them by playing games that give us power? Open and honest communication can strengthen a relationship because it lets each partner look at the issues that are contributing to their unconscious reactions. **One of the functions of a loving relationship is to help both persons free themselves from habitual patterns that do not serve them.**

AGGRESSIVE VS. PASSIVE

Often, we respond to someone in an aggressive way because it gives us a feeling of control over a situation that makes us uncomfortable. A lot of kids are aggressive because they don't want others to be in charge of them or to take advantage of them. But who really has control when you get angry, you or the other person? My experience is that when I get angry, the other person has control over me. He or she is controlling my mood. As far as anger giving you power, any martial arts instructor will tell you that it's easy to defeat a person when they are angry.

There are many ways that responding aggressively can backfire as a way of communicating. Some people think that screaming their feelings is a surefire way to be heard but, in fact, it's usually a way to make others tune you out. A third grade teacher in one of my workshops offered a good example. She shared a story about two elementary school students, Maci and Alyssa, who were always arguing at lunchtime. During one of these arguments the teacher approached Maci, who was very upset and started yelling as she told her version of what had happened.

"When this happens, I often react by telling Maci very harshly not to yell in my face. This time I chose to employ a different tactic by stopping her and explaining that I could not listen to her when she spoke like that. When she began again she was still very hostile and loud. I stopped her again and expressed to her how I felt when she yelled. I further explained to everyone else involved that if they wanted people to give a positive response to what they were saying, they would have to say it in a way that was not offensive to the person trying to listen. I told Maci that I would listen when she was ready to speak to me in a more respectful manner. She took a moment or two to collect herself and then explained what had happened in a calmer tone. I felt that her relaxed tone helped, in part, to defuse the situation."

On the other end of the spectrum are people who react passively. Passive types generally try to resolve conflict by not saying anything. They might back down during an argument or not speak up for themselves if they feel they're being mistreated. Some kids are passive in other ways. They might get straight A's on their homework and quizzes but they never raise their hand in class to answer a question. Often they don't share because they are afraid of being wrong or bringing attention to themselves. Many of these children have the intelligence and discipline to be leaders but this won't happen until they develop the courage to speak their truth.

Once we understand and can observe our habitual patterns of communication, we can choose which pattern serves us the best in any given situation. The assertive approach is preferable in most situations, but for those of us who are habitually aggressive, a little passivity can go a long way. Likewise, for a passive person, choosing to get angry every once in a while may be just fine. Whatever your habitual mode of communication, the goal is to step back, observe and then choose what works best in any given situation.

DO YOU WANT PEACE OR WAR?

To understand how powerful we are as creators, think of two prizefighters. If Lenox Lewis is scheduled to fight Mike Tyson on March 1 and Tyson says on February 28 that he is not going to fight, will there be a fight? No, there won't. We all share the same power to decide whether there will be peace or war in each moment of our lives.

One student summed up the lesson on communication by saying, "The most valuable thing I learned from the course is that I can be assertive without hurting others and without the fear of being disliked. Discovering that I have a choice to respond to hurt in a fashion that makes war or peace has totally changed how I relate to others."

COMMUNICATION

1. OBSERVE YOUR HABITUAL MODE OF COMMUNICATION WITH YOUR CHILD, SPOUSE, CO-WORKER OR ANY OTHER SIGNIFICANT PERSON. RECORD THE CHANGES YOU MAKE WHEN YOUR COMMUNICATION BECOMES ASSERTIVE RATHER THAN AGGRESSIVE OR PASSIVE.

   • Changes made

   • Result of changes

2. OBSERVE AND RECORD YOUR PATTERN OF GETTING ANGRY WHEN YOU DON'T GET WHAT YOU WANT. THIS CAN OCCUR AT A RED LIGHT, WHEN A PERSON SAYS "NO" TO YOU OR IN MANY OTHER SITUATIONS.

DO YOU WANT WAR OR PEACE?

PARTICIPANTS' COMMENTS

- Since taking the course, a woman shared that she had learned more beneficial ways to approach issues that come up with her daughter. However, she was still having difficulty communicating with her husband and was afraid that if she spoke her truth it would create conflict and she "did not want to make waves". I told her that the price we pay for not making waves is a loss of vitality and less then optimal health. Withholding our truth is a major cause of illness and feeling unhappy. She was encouraged to communicate her true feelings to her husband.

- A teacher shared in her homework: "I see a change in my approach towards Delfin (one of her students). I was habitually aggressive with him. After our class on choices in communication, I find myself using a more assertive approach. For example, a week ago, if Delfin asked to borrow a pencil I would have aggressively repri- manded him for not being prepared for class. But now I reflect for a second or two and use a kinder, more assertive approach before lending him the pencil.

    At this point I believe he may be a little confused with my behavior, but I feel less stress when using this assertive approach."

- A mother shared, "Friday I asked my mom to be ready to go the hairdresser. When I arrived she was not ready which was going to make me late for my appointment. I would normally yell and be very aggressive with her because of her inconsiderateness. What I did differently was that when my mom came into the car, I informed her that the next time she made me late for an appointment, she would have to find another means of transportation. I said this in an assertive non-threatening way."

- In speaking about an assistant teacher who was constantly disre- specting her, another teacher commented, "I have created this problem with my assistant teacher because if I had been assertive in my interaction with her, she would have been aware that I do not like what has been going on. But since I decided to be passive, I promoted the situation and she took advantage of it. I have learned that it is better to address an issue rather than to pretend that it does not exist. I have now decided not to take any action of hers for granted but to tell her what I think about anything she does that affects me emotionally."

DO YOU WANT WAR OR PEACE?

EMOTIONAL UNDERSTANDING

More than any other factor, a child's skills in managing his emotions will determine his level of achievement in life.

Dealing with children during times of emotional turmoil and conflict is one of the most stressful aspects of parenting. In this chapter, we will present specific steps to guide you through these potentially difficult times and help you to coach your child through emotional upheaval.

WHAT DO YOU DO WHEN YOUR CHILD IS BLUE?

Parents who have taken the time to participate in the Masterful Parenting program are motivated by a loving and caring attitude toward their children. However, loving and caring, although extremely important, are not enough; they are only the necessary first steps toward a fulfilling relationship with our children. With caring as our foundation, we have experienced increased growth as we have explored and become better at listening, taking responsibility, forgiving, accepting and communicating. But there is still another level of mastery that is necessary for success as a parent: knowing how to coach our children when emotions run hot. Many parents who are loving and caring have attitudes about their own as well as their children's emotions that prevent effective communication when their child is experiencing negative or tumultuous feelings.

According to researcher Dr. John Gotman, parents fall into two broad categories with regard to their responses to their children's emotional upset. Parents in one category give guidance and coach their children when emotions run hot. The others do not. The first group, whom Gotman calls *emotion coaches*, view feelings such as fear, anger and sadness as opportunities for children to learn valuable life lessons. They are able to accept their children's feelings and patiently help them to find creative solutions to their problems. Further on in this chapter we will discuss emotion coaching in greater depth. But first, let's look at the parents who are not able to provide support and guidance when children are experiencing negative emotions.

Dismissive Parents want to make the world perfect and believe that their children are never supposed to be sad. They pamper them and don't acknowledge or discuss negative emotions, such as fear and anger. They often don't show their own emotions because they are afraid that their own anger might devastate someone. Instead of empathizing with their children's emotional outbursts, they refer to them as cute or comment, "Don't be so upset, it's not that big a deal."

Disapproving Parents are often critical and lack empathy for their children's negative emotions. They regard anger or crying as a form of manipulation. Obedience is their main concern. These parents often punish a boy for expressing fear or require a daughter to swallow her anger.

Laissez-faire Parents are similar to parents who coach their children, in that they accept all feelings. The difference lies in their inability to give guidance while a child is experiencing negative or turbulent emotions. These are the overly permissive parents who often do not set adequate boundaries for their children.

THE EMOTION COACH

Emotion coaches, according to Gotmen, guide and counsel their children toward solutions to their problems. They don't try to "fix" everything but instead focus on the potential for learning from the experiences that emotional storms can provide. They value being real and are not afraid to apologize when they handle a situation poorly. They show emotions in front of their children. They are aware that children can learn about the staying power of relationships by observing arguments and then seeing them resolved. These parents set limits and relate consequences to actions. Research has shown that children of these Parental Masters:

- Get along better with, show more affection to and feel less tension around their parents.

- Are less prone to becoming upset and when they do become upset, recover more quickly.

- Are more relaxed, as indicated by lower levels of stress hormones.

- Are more popular with their peers and more highly regarded by their teachers.

- Are more attentive and learn more effectively.

- Have higher achievement scores in math and reading by the time they reach the third grade.

These children exemplify positive attributes not because of obedience and forced compliance but because they feel connected to their parents through empathy and understanding.

If we multiply these results, we can see how transformation will occur on a significant societal level as more children are coached by Masterful Parents – parents who demonstrate forgiveness, acceptance, reflection and responsibility in their lives while relating to their children in a compassionate, trusting and loving way. This is not a fantasy, but a reality that can occur through education, training, practice and will.

The six basic steps for emotion coaching apply the wisdom gained from the previous chapters.

1. **WE BECOME CLEAR ABOUT OUR INTENTION.** The intention of an emotion coach is to use the child's emotional outburst as an opportunity for guidance and intimacy. This is a very different intention from using the display of negative emotions as an opportunity to make our child wrong, deny his experience or punish him. Getting clear about our intention in any situation goes a long way towards fulfilling our desires.

2. **WE BECOME AWARE OF AND RESPONSIBLE FOR THE SPECIFIC EMOTIONS WE ARE EXPERIENCING.** Once we acknowledge what we are feeling, we need to take responsibility for how we feel. I demonstrate this in class by asking one of the participants to call me a liar. We then discuss the various responses I could choose, such as calmly stating, "I am not a liar," or angrily threatening "Who are you calling a liar?" or "I may have lied in the past but I'm not lying now." Who determines my response to being called a liar? I do. **Our children don't make us angry, upset or sad. We are the source of what we feel.**

3. **WE LISTEN WITH AN EMPATHETIC HEART.** This is the most important quality of an emotion coach. As we feel what the other is feeling, we become an ally for our children. For this to happen, we must listen and do nothing else. We must be able to hear, accept and not want to change what our child is feeling. We must embrace our child's sadness, whininess, anger, crying, impatience, disappointment and frustration. Not an easy task, but remember, we are talking about mastery here.

4. **WE ASSIST OUR CHILD IN IDENTIFYING AND COMMUNICATING THE EMOTIONS HE IS FEELING.** By prompting with questions, we help the child to verbalize his emotional state (e.g. I feel angry, sad, bored, tired, afraid, confused, tense, etc.). Of course, the response depends on the child's age but I have heard very young children give articulate answers when encouraged to describe their feelings.

5. **WE RECOGNIZE AND ACKNOWELEDGE OUR CHILD'S UNFULFILLED NEEDS.** Often, we become upset when our need for love, joy, safety, appreciation, freedom or cooperation is not being met. Family conflicts often arise when our children's need for freedom, independence and self expression challenges our need for their safety. This is a common cause of contention with our teenager, and is

first encountered as the habitual "no" of our two-year-old as she attempts to assert her own identity.

Communication that acknowledges both party's needs and feelings, rather than negatively judging our own as well as our child's needs, goes a long way towards peacefully resolving these types of situations. Shouting, "I can't take this anymore. How many times do I have to tell you to be home on time. You're grounded forever," is one way of communicating your displeasure. Another way, which honors needs and choice, is stating, "I recognize your need to go out with your friends and be independent. I have the need to know that you are safe. How can we satisfy both our needs?"

In a similar situation, that all parents can relate to, you may recognize this voice: "This room is a pig sty. I am sick and tired of telling you to clean up your room. Aren't you ashamed of yourself?" Instead, you may want to try this one: "I have a need for cooperation, appreciation, and a neat house. When you don't clean up your room, I feel as if you don't care," This communication honors our needs and also teaches our children to honor and express their needs.

6. **WE SUPPORT OUR CHILD IN HER ATTEMPT TO FIND A SOLUTIONS TO HER PROBLEMS.** This process begins with asking her what she thinks would be the best solution. Then we go on to discuss alternative solutions. Questions such as: "How would you feel if you were in his place?" "What have been the consequences when you have acted that way?" and "What can you do toward best serve yourself and the other people involved?" go a long way to bringing peace and fulfillment back into our children's lives. We must always keep in mind that as parents we must set limits. Children need to realize that all emotions – but not all behaviors – are acceptable. After a consideration of all the consequences of each choice, we can encourage our child to pick one solution.

AGAIN, WE TEACH WHO WE ARE

The six steps for being an emotion coach can only be effective in the hands of parents who are skillful in managing their own feelings. Once again, the emphasis is "we teach who we are."

Virtually all parents are deeply attuned to the emotional lives of their children. When our 10-year-old walks in the door crying because he was not chosen for the baseball team we feel that pain. We have no choice, the connection is that strong. The choice comes when we decide how we respond to that pain. The dismissive parent would tend to minimize their child's pain and just try to ignore him or tell him to "pull yourself together." On the other hand, the disapproving parent would have no tolerance and not allow the emotion to continue and discourage the child from expressing those emotions again.

The root of the inability to establish an empathetic connection can be found in our own upbringing. If our parents were not emotion coaches how were we to learn how to manage our feelings? If our parents were afraid of or not in control of their own emotions then emotions may seem as threatening to us as they were to them. However, we owe it to our children and ourselves to explore other more beneficial ways of managing our feelings. By being open enough to consider the possibility of becoming an emotion coach, you have come a long way already. We must be patient with ourselves in acquiring the skills we need in order to be the teacher our child deserves.

Our emotional health is determined mainly by the quality of the intimate relationships that surround us. When parents nurture and support one another, the child's ability to resolve upset is greatly enhanced. Research has shown that children living in environments where parents are critical, hostile and show contempt for each other are likely to have problems managing their own emotions, tend to be aggressive and have more problems getting along with others. Even divorce in itself is not as detrimental to a child's well being as is the way couples relate to each other while they are together or after a divorce. Although this chapter focuses on our interaction with our children, the steps for managing emotional upset and resolving conflict are also meant to be used internally and with any appropriate person in our lives. Using every opportunity available to make us a more conscious human being will make us more masterful parents.

The next homework assignment is to be done over a three-week period. Its purpose is to demonstrate the power that intention, taking responsibility and taking action have as agents of transformation in our lives.

THE RELATIONSHIP PROJECT

1. FOR THE NEXT THREE WEEKS, WHO DO YOU WANT TO FOCUS ON AND SIGNIFICANTLY IMPROVE YOUR RELATIONSHIP WITH?

2. LIST SPECIFIC AREAS THAT YOU WOULD LIKE TO IMPROVE.

114

3. WRITE ABOUT THE EFFECTS OF THE STEPS OR INTERVENTIONS YOU TOOK IN ORDER TO IMPROVE YOUR RELATIONSHIP WITH THE PERSON YOU CHOSE.

Examples of outer interventions:

- Writing a letter to the person

- Taking them out to dinner, a movie, etc. Giving them something that shows you care

- Communicating lovingly once a day

- Telling them how much you appreciate them i.e. *gratitude*

- Clearing up areas of your life that are incomplete with them i.e. *communication*

- Observing patterns of communication that may not serve your relationship (e.g., aggressive or passive behavior) and making changes

Examples of inner intervention:

- Getting in touch with and forgiving yourself for any judgment you have against the other person. (Do this at least three times a day.)

- Thinking of them lovingly – See the person with a smile on their face everyday.

- At least once a day, visualize what it would look like to have a good relationship with this person.

4. **RECORD WHAT CHANGES YOU OBSERVED IN YOUR RELATIONSHIP WHEN YOU TOOK INTERNAL ACTIONS BASED ON PRINCIPLES THAT WE HAVE EXPLORED:**

- Taking responsibility (create, promote, or allow)

- Acceptance

- Choice

- Forgiveness

5. RATE FROM 1-10 YOUR LEVEL OF SATISFACTION WITH YOUR RELATIONSHIP BEFORE DOING THIS ASSIGNMENT AND AGAIN AFTER ITS COMPLETION.

6. WHAT SPECIFIC LESSONS HAVE YOU INCORPORATED INTO YOUR RELATIONSHIP WITH YOUR CHILDREN? FRIENDS? RELATIVES?

10

PRACTICING POSITIVE DISCIPLINE THROUGH THE UNDERSTANDING OF OUR CHILD'S TEMPERAMENT

The more awareness and empathy we bring to understanding our children's behavior, the better able we are to guide them in a positive direction.

A person's temperament is not the same as his or her personality. It is but one part of the personality along with intelligence, emotion and sense of humor. Temperament is the distinguishing style or characteristic that makes someone's personality unique. It is normal for each individual to bring a distinct set of behavior patterns to various situations. These patterns are a reflection of that person's temperament.

Approximately half a child's temperament is inherited, explains William B. Carey, M.D., in his book *Understanding Your Child's Temperament*. The other half is determined by a combination of physical, psychological and environmental factors such as conditions during the mother's pregnancy (e.g., nutrition, drug use or general health), the child's physical health after birth and the influence of the family. Parents need to recognize the inborn nature of temperament since many problems in parenting come from trying to work against and change the child's natural behavioral style. **Parents cannot change their child's basic temperament. However, they can alter and control the way they respond to and manage it.**

Until this point, we have focused on how a parent's behavior affects the child. We are now dealing with the importance of the parent-child interaction. This is where the principles of acceptance and how you relate to the issue is the issue come into play. Given that your child's temperament is basically pre-determined, how you relate to and accept that temperament can either support or disrupt the interaction you have with your child. In essence, how you feel about and adapt to your child's temperament are as important as the temperament itself.

Dr. Carey describes nine traits that blend together to determine a child's unique, largely inborn temperament. Understanding these traits can help you to become more accepting of your child's individuality. Ideally, you should observe them in various settings at different times. For instance when observing the "activity" trait, look for fidgeting while eating, reading, watching TV and standing on line.

ACTIVITY

This characteristic refers to physical motion during sleep, play, work, eating, dressing, bathing and other daily activities. Does the child usually sit still or squirm around and fidget? The tendency to be more active and engaged in one's surroundings should not be confused with hyperactivity which tends to be disorganized and without purpose.

REGULARITY

This trait determines how predictable a child's responses will be to the events in his or her daily life. For young children, it can be observed in their cycle of sleeping, eating and elimination. In older children this trait manifests itself in behavior such as completing tasks on schedule, the amount of food routinely consumed at meals and the consistency of snack time.

INITIAL REACTION

This is how your child initially responds to new people, situations, places, food, toys and procedures. At one end of the spectrum is the child who accepts and approaches ordinary degrees of novelty with little hesitation. At the other end is the shy, timid child who does not engage in new situations or withdraws from them entirely, at least for a while.

ADAPTABILITY

Adaptability is the adjustment over the long term that follows the initial response. It shows a range between flexibility and rigidity in adjusting to the environment after the child's first reaction. For instance, if one parent usually gives the child a bath, observe how quickly the child adapts if the other takes over.

INTENSITY

Intensity is the measure of how much energy your child puts into his or her responses, regardless of whether the response is positive and happy or negative and fussy. A more intense child will be more physically active and louder in his or her responses while a placid child will show less expression of feeling and physical motion.

MOOD

A child's predominant mood can be positive, negative, or somewhere in between. To better assess your child's predisposition for mood, look for an overall pattern that occurs in various situations.

PERSISTENCE AND ATTENTION SPAN

Persistence refers to a child's inclination to stick with an activity despite obstacles or interruptions. Attention span is demonstrated by how long a child continues an activity or pursues a task when there are no interruptions.

DISTRACTIBILITY

Some children are easily distracted by noise, light, sounds or other people, whereas other children have no problem tuning out stimuli. A child's level of distractibility does not necessarily affect his or her persistence because a child can be very easily distracted yet still return immediately to a task and stick with it until is finished.

SENSITIVITY

Sensitivity refers to the amount of stimulation from factors such as noise, sights, smells and lights needed to arouse a response. All five senses give clues to a child's sensitivity trait. For example, how does your child respond to tight or itchy clothing, a change in a familiar person's appearance or foods with strong or mild flavors?

Some of these categories tend to cluster together. For instance, many shy children have a slow initial response, are less adaptable, have lower intensity of response, are less physically active and experience more negative moods. Similarly, the "easy" cluster of traits describes children who are pleasant, flexible, not too intense and fairly predictable.

Also, be aware that the child's age can affect the constancy of the temperament he or she exhibits. Temperament does not begin to stabilize until a child is three or four months old and may be harder to gauge in newborns. During adolescence, factors such as hormones, dietary eccentricities, sleep deprivation, rigorous athletic training and the use of drugs or alcohol can influence a teenager's temperament. Also, by this age youngsters can alter their temperament to "fit" with their peers. For instance, a youth may push herself forward in spite of feeling timid and having a shy temperament. Although the expression may be different, the feelings are still there.

TEMPERAMENT AND STRESS

In school age children, the traits that influence development the most are persistence, attention span and adaptability. In fact, a child's temperament seems to contribute more to test results than I.Q. For example, teachers' ratings of high attention span, high persistence, low distractibility and low activity among elementary school students were shown to relate to better performance on standardized achievement tests in reading and mathematics. Likewise, the traits of low persistence, high distractibility, high activity, shyness, low adaptability and negative mood often contributed to poorer classroom performance.

Research has shown that eight of the nine more challenging traits were significantly associated with the development of stress: high activity, low adaptability, withdrawal from new stimuli, distractibility, high intensity, negative mood, low persistence and irregularity. A study of 155 normal six- to nine-year-old children found a correlation between high levels of stress and behavioral problems. For example, children with low adaptability and high intensity are much less likely to adjust to a newborn sibling or the divorce of their parents and as a result, will experience elevated levels of stress.

ADAPTING TO YOUR CHILD'S TEMPERAMENT

How you react to your child's temperament not only affects the parent-child interaction but also can have a positive or negative impact on your daily functioning. Personal relationships, work performance, self-assurance, and various aspects of mental and bodily functions, such as eating and sleeping, are effected by how we relate to our children. It affects our self-esteem and our competence as parents when we allow our inability to accept and cope to produce frustration, anger and guilt. Our child's positive temperament traits can make us feel successful as parents, whereas having to deal with a difficult child can make us feel totally ineffective.

Some parents may find it easy to relate to their children. It's much easier to parent a child who easily accepts and adapts to new things whereas a child with a more resistant temperament can frustrate even the calmest parents leaving them stressed and feeling incompetent. Similarly, intense, high-spirited, persistent children can be exhausting to supervise. And a child who is stubborn, who frowns, sulks, protests and is abrasive is much harder to be warm to than a child who is friendly, upbeat, pays attention to requests and rarely complains.

We need to observe the impact that our child's temperament has on us. Which traits please you, and which can bother you or cause friction within your family? For example, a very active child may delight very athletic parents but totally unnerve parents who lead a quiet, sedentary life.

Gender can also affect how we relate to a trait. Shyness is traditionally more acceptable in girls than in boys, whereas high activity is usually not as well accepted in girls as it is in boys. Certain traits may be easier to accept in one phase of our child's development but deemed negative in another. For instance, a young child who adapts easily to new people and environments is regarded with a great deal of parental acceptance. However, this same trait in adolescence can lead to experimentation with drugs, alcohol, tobacco and other types of risky behavior.

The following chart, from Dr. William B. Carey's *Understanding Your Child's Temperament* illustrates the positive and negative aspects of different character traits and how they can affect the parent-child relationship.

TRAIT	SOMETIME NEGATIVE ASPECTS	GENERALLY POSITIVE ASPECTS
Activity	**High:** Social activities and task performance are easily interfered with. May be mislabeled "hyperactive." Hyperactivity is disorganized, purposeless activity and not simply high activity. **Low:** Slow to perform tasks; may seem drowsy; may be labeled "lazy."	**High:** Vigorous and energetic; explores surroundings; stays active in dull environments. **Low:** Less disruptive in cramped environments and circumstances.
Regularity	**High:** May be a problem if the environment cannot provide for needs on schedule. **Low:** Unpredictable care requirements.	**High:** Few surprises for parents and other caregivers. **Low:** May not be bothered by irregularities in caregiving or routine events.
Initial reaction	**Approaching or bold:** May accept negative influences too quickly, which is dangerous in hazardous environments. **Withdrawing or inhibited:** Slow to accept change; may avoid useful experiences.	**Approaching or bold:** Makes a rapid fit in favorable settings. **Withdrawing or inhibited:** Cautious in dangerous situations e.g. in accepting offers from strangers.
Adaptability	**High:** In danger of accepting negative influences, such as antisocial values of peers. **Low:** May have difficulty adjusting to requirements of caregiving; stress-producing; may be labeled "difficult."	**High:** Generally at an advantage; accepts positive influences more quickly; in greater harmony with caregivers. **Low:** Less likely to accept negative influences.

TRAIT	SOMETIME NEGATIVE ASPECTS	GENERALLY POSITIVE ASPECTS
Intensity	**High:** Abrasive and annoying; may evoke counterintensity; may mislead parents or other caregivers as to seriousness of an issue or illness. **Low:** Needs may not be expressed with enough forcefulness to be recognized.	**High:** Needs are certain to get attention; caregivers welcome the positive intensity. **Low:** Easier to live with.
Mood	**Positive:** May be too positive and upbeat about real problems. **Negative:** Unpleasant for parents and other caregivers, who may overestimate importance of issue or physical complaint.	**Positive:** Welcome. **Negative:** Few advantages; however, may evoke more positive involvement from parents and other caregivers because of their concerns.
Persistence and attention span	**High:** Being absorbed in work and play may make the child seem to ignore parents, teachers, etc. **Low:** Less efficient at task performances; fails to perform as expected. Not to be considered an "attention-deficit" if the child functions well, particularly in combination with compensatory factors such as high adaptability and intelligence.	**High:** Greater achievement likely at various tasks and school performance. **Low:** May be more easily drawn out of activities or habits that are unacceptable to parents and other caregivers.
Distractibility	**High:** Easily diverted from tasks; performance is easily interfered with; needs reminders. **Low:** May be unaware of important signals, such as warnings from parents.	**High:** Easy to soothe as an infant. **Low:** Can work efficiently in noisy places.

TRAIT	SOMETIME NEGATIVE ASPECTS	GENERALLY POSITIVE ASPECTS
Sensitivity	**High:** More perceptive of surrounding noises, smells, lights, textures, and internal sensations; as an infant, more prone to colic and sleep disturbances. **Low:** May miss important cues from surroundings.	**High:** More aware of changes in environment and of existence and nuances of other peoples' thoughts and feelings. **Low:** More shielded from too much environmental input.

You cannot change a child's temperament. You cannot hammer the undesirable traits out of children with rigid discipline, bribery or attempts at reasonable persuasion. What you can do is learn to accept those traits and at the same time develop alternative ways to manage your child's temperament to reduce stress and maximize harmonious interaction.

125

PRACTICAL SUGGESTIONS FOR
EFFECTIVELY MANAGING SPECIFIC TRAITS

ACTIVITY

Active children need outlets for their energy and the opportunity for physical motion while also needing to be taught about boundaries. For example, if you plan to go shopping with a very active child, the child should have a chance to be active before going shopping but also told beforehand that running around in the store is not permitted.

By contrast, children who are low in activity need more time to complete tasks. They are often judged as "lazy" and do not perform well on standardized tests. Sometimes we can speed up these children without criticizing them. For instance they could be given a kitchen timer or hourglass as a way of keeping them in touch with a time requirement.

REGULARITY

Children high in regularity are very predictable and have no problem following routine schedules but they can become very upset if schedules are changed at the last minute. A way to deal with this is to give as much advance notice as possible before making changes. Also, being very loving and nurturing when explaining changes to routine scheduling is a way of respecting this trait and encouraging more adaptability in the future.

Children with low regularity have trouble keeping to schedules. From the toddler years on, parents can impose regular mealtimes and bedtimes however, they must not insist that the child be hungry or tired at the exact appointed hour. The child should not be criticized for this trait, but should be expected to join the family at mealtime whether she is hungry or not. They should also be complimented and/or rewarded for being early or on time in various situations. When considering a day care center or school for this type of child look for one with a loosely organized schedule.

INITIAL REACTION

Entering unfamiliar territory is easy for children whose initial reaction is positive or outgoing. They enjoy meeting new people and exploring new places. These children should be told that it is good to be friendly, but to be wary of strangers. Younger children should be constantly told not to go with anyone they don't know.

On the other hand, parents should not punish a child whose initial response to novelty is withdrawal. Offering gentle encouragement and preparing them for a new experience in advance is usually more effective than coercion or forced compliance.

ADAPTABILITY

The flexibility that a child displays in accepting change should not be taken for granted but encouraged as often as possible. The only downside to a high level of adaptability can be a willingness to embody negative ideas and concepts from peers, the internet or television. Parents should be cautious and monitor their child's exposure to possible negative influences.

Children with low adaptability usually just require extra time, preparation or advance warning in order to adjust. For example, if you are planning a trip to the beach for the first time, weeks beforehand you can show your child pictures of the beach, buy a sand bucket and answer any questions your child may have.

INTENSITY

Children with high intensity seem to operate consistently at a higher volume. Their loud, dramatic responses don't always mean that their position is emotionally charged or that they're unwilling to compromise. It's just their way of communicating. With these youngsters parents are better off responding in a composed, even and understanding tone rather than trying to match the child's level of intensity.

The parent of the low intensity child needs to realize that feelings and thoughts expressed unemotionally in a low voice may be as important to this child as those expressed loudly by more intense children. For example, the child may be experiencing strong physical discomfort caused by an illness but never utter a word, whereas the high intensity child might cry and scream, causing you to call an ambulance for a problem that does not warrant such extreme measures.

MOOD

Some children simply don't come into this life with sunny dispositions. Parents can help older children reduce a tendency toward negativity by giving them nurturing suggestions such as, "Johnny might respond more nicely to you if you went out of your way and were nice to him first." Being patient and not trying to constantly persuade the child to cheer up can go a long way to helping the child see the world in a brighter light.

PERSISTENCE AND ATTENTION SPAN

These traits have tremendous advantages for a student or adult but can be very challenging in dealing with a young child. Persistent children often get so involved with projects that they forget to play and just have fun. Parents need to encourage these youngsters to be "lighter" and play more.

The opposite scenario occurs with children who manifest a low persistence trait or are easily distracted. They are less likely to follow through on homework and household tasks. Dividing long tasks into smaller segments with breaks in between can help less persistent or less attentive children complete their assignments.

DISTRACTIBILITY

With infants, it's a blessing when the child is easily distracted and soothed by mobiles or by being picked up. But parents may have to be more creative in finding ways to distract and soothe youngsters whose attention is not easily diverted.

For adolescents, a tendency toward becoming distracted can be disruptive. These children should not be allowed to have the television or radio on while they are doing homework and should have a quiet room where they can study without interruption. Also, when having a discussion with a child who loses focus easily, it is wise to do so in a place that is quiet and free from distractions. On the other hand, there are some adolescents who can actually study better and retain more information listening to music or the television while doing their homework.

SENSITIVITY

Highly sensitive children are more aware of and more reactive to changes in their environment. These children can irritate others with their heightened sensitivity but in reality they are simply more attuned to what is going on around them. Parents should avoid placing negative labels such as "finicky," "complainer" or "difficult" on these children. Likewise, parents of low sensitivity children should be aware of the tendency to label these children as "slow" or "not aware".

TEMPERAMENT AND BEHAVIORAL PROBLEMS 129

Temperament can be a cause of behavioral problems when it conflicts with the values and expectations of parents or other caregivers. Researchers found that when parents responded poorly to the "difficult" trait cluster of low adaptability, withdrawing initial reaction, negative mood, high intensity and irregularity, the child often responded by behaving in an inappropriate fashion. Ask yourself: Could my pushing my shy child too hard be the cause of his resistance to getting out of the car and walking into school? Could my child's rebellion against the new second-grade teacher stem from her demands that all children adjust to her rigid program? Could my child's constant acting out in class be due to the lack of physical movement and exercise allowed by her teacher? Could my badgering my child to be more upbeat contribute to her not wanting to go anywhere with me? Could imposing a rigid time schedule on my child be causing her to rebel by never being on time?

It is not the "difficult" traits themselves that cause the problem, rather, it is the way that the caregivers and teachers respond to these traits. I'm not suggesting that you surrender your authority – I'm asking you to be creative and look for alternative approaches that take your child's temperament into consideration. **Work with your child's temperament, not against it.**

Similarly, children with learning disabilities have normal temperaments just like children without learning disabilities – the behavioral problems often occur when parents do not alter their interaction to produce a better "fit" with these traits and temperaments of these children. Many adolescents diagnosed with ADHD (Attention Deficit Hyperactivity Disorder) are exhibiting normal temperaments that are "difficult" to deal with. The ADHD diagnosis has failed to recognize that half of normal children are more active, more inattentive or more distractible than average. Russell A. Barkley, Ph.D., author of *Taking Charge of ADHD: The Complete Authoritative Guide for Parents*, states that the common problem with children diagnosed with ADHD is self-regulation, or a low adaptability temperament. **Do the ten percent of children today who are being diagnosed as ADHD really all have brain abnormalities, or is the diagnosis in part, a reflection of society's inability to deal with the temperament traits of low adaptability, low attentiveness, high distractibility and high activity?**

PRACTICING POSITIVE DISCIPLINE

With the understanding of temperament as a foundation, we can now approach discipline with more compassion and understanding. Simply listening is an effective way parents can manage a difficult child. Reflecting a moment before responding, rather than acting on impulse is another way of showing your child you care. Both strategies show a concerted effort on your part to understand your child's point of view.

Once you have heard their particular point of view, do you make them a participant in the decision making process, or use power to enforce your position? Use of power fosters deep resentment; young children who submit to severe punishment often become more rebellious as adolescents. Using power to control may work early on, but we are concerned with the best approach for the long run.

In his book *Taking Charge of ADHD*, Dr. Barkley offers several techniques for managing undesirable behavior when dealing with ADHD. These suggestions are applicable to unruly children as well as those with challenging temperament qualities:

POSITIVE REINFORCEMENT

Rewarding children for good behavior and fining them for overstepping boundaries can be a very effective way of establishing new behavior patterns. **Difficult children require more powerful positive consequences than children with easier temperaments.** Depending on the child's age you may want to reward good behavior with tokens or a monetary allowance. For instance, dressing quickly before school, making the bed or doing homework after dinner can be rewarded with five tokens whereas brushing teeth, not fighting with siblings at dinner and putting clothes away can be rewarded with two tokens. Similarly, you can fine your child for not obeying established guidelines or following through on promises. But be careful about using too many fines – **you should focus more on rewarding positive behavior than penalizing your child for stepping out of bounds.** Also, (if using a token system) be sure to determine the value of the tokens so the child knows what they are worth. For example, watching television for 30 minutes could cost five tokens while special rewards like going to the movies could be worth 200 tokens.

A reward system approach may make life easier but another approach brings a family into more loving cooperation. This occurs when children do their chores and contribute to the family from an attitude of understanding, joy and desire rather than from a feeling of obligation or fear of consequences. One way to achieve this is to have children participate in creating household rules. Labeling them "agreements" or "expectations" is a step in the right direction. Likewise, having a discussion based on the question, "What consequences do you think are reasonable for a specific action?" empowers your children by making them part of the decision making process. Considering your child's point of view creates an environment of mutual respect. For example, before your adolescent son goes out on a Saturday night with his friends, knowing that there is an 11:00 p.m. curfew, you might ask: "If you choose not to come home on time, what do you think the consequences should be?"

Another "masterful" approach is to look at the cause of negative behavior in a specific situation rather than just focusing on the appropriate consequence (punishment) for that action. For instance, your eight-year-old daughter usually gets irritable and whiny after dinner, just before it's time for her to sit down and do her homework. Your point of view could be, "if you continue to whine, you will not be allowed to watch TV before going to bed for one week." But, in reality, her irritability is an allergic reaction to the glass of milk she drank with her dinner. Having the willingness to explore at a deeper level by asking "why" rather than immediately taking punitive action goes a long way toward strengthening the bond between parents and their children and creates an environment where the child feels like a true "member" of the family.

WORK BEFORE FUN

132

A similar type of punishment-reward strategy, called the Primack principle, is to deny your child access to more enjoyable activities until less-fun or necessary work is done. For example, tell your child that he or she can only watch television after the dishes are done. This turns ordinary activities into privileges that must be earned.

MANAGING ATTENTION SPAN

Because temperamental children (children with difficult temperaments) often have shorter attention spans and are more easily distracted, it can help to split homework into more manageable segments. For instance, you can request that your child do 15 minutes of homework when he or she comes home, 15 minutes before dinner, and 15 minutes after dinner. Also, encourage your child to do homework in areas of the house that work best for his or her study habits. Your child may need to take frequent breaks or vary activities and music could either help or hinder the child's ability to concentrate. **Certain foods may also detract from your child's ability to concentrate. Be aware of allergens, such as preservatives, wheat, dairy and sugar.**

FREQUENT FEEDBACK

Frequent feedback, especially positive feedback, is far more effective than punishment with temperamental children. Use punishment only after frequent feedback and incentives fail not to change a negative behavior.

TIME OUTS

Calling "time out" can be a good strategy if your young child does not respond to two repeated requests. **A time out should not be viewed as punishment but, instead, as a break taken by you and your child in order to restore a more balanced and loving interaction.** State your request firmly but not angrily. If your child does not respond or says "no," wait five seconds, and then repeat the request. Then tell your child that she will have to sit in a chair for a minimum of two minutes if she doesn't obey. (A good time formula is to penalize the child with a minimum of one or two minutes for each year of age.) Wait another five seconds. Then, if she still refuses to comply, send the child to the time out. Once the minimum sentence is over, wait for her to be quiet for 30 seconds. Now she must agree to comply with your original request or apologize if she said something mean or inappropriate. As soon as she agrees, be sure to give praise for the cooperation. If she still refuses to comply, use the time out strategy again.

FAIR PLAY

Parents should spend time teaching a difficult child how to play with other children in a positive, non-aggressive fashion. Talk about and define specific behaviors that are desirable as well as those that aren't appreciated when relating to friends. While your child is interacting with his peers, constantly remind him of the desired behavior and offer positive reinforcement when he acts appropriately. Other helpful strategies are to encourage your child's friends to come to play at your house, discourage competition and not allow out of control friends to play with your child. But beyond all techniques, the most powerful influence on your child's interaction with his or her peers is the type of behavior you model in your home.

PREPARATION

If you know that your child usually demonstrates negative behavior in certain situations, prepare in advance to reduce the likelihood of a disagreement. For instance, before entering a restaurant talk to your child about the type of behavior you expect, along with the punishment or rewards that he can expect depending upon his behavior. Temperamental children respond poorly to pressure. The best form of motivation is praise and encouragement rather than pressure in the heat of the moment.

CLEAR COMMUNICATION

Instead of asking a question, present commands in a direct fashion. For example, "please pick up that towel" is far more effective than, "do you want to pick up that towel?" After giving the command, give immediate feedback based on your child's response. For example, if the child does not respond to your request, restate the command and be prepared to ask for a time out. Similarly, if the child obeys, be sure to say "thank you" and show your appreciation.

CREDIBILITY

This means that if you say there will be consequences or that you will not tolerate a certain type of behavior, be firm and don't give in. For instance, children often whine to get attention. When your daughter starts whining, you can say, "Stop whining". When she stops you can say, "thank you". If she starts whining again, don't give her any attention until she stops. This is difficult but over time if you don't give in she will see that whining doesn't work as an attention-getting mechanism.

FAMILY MEETIING

In many households, regularly scheduled family meetings have become the forum for discussing important issues and concerns. The following guidelines are the foundation for a successful family meeting:

- Meetings should be scheduled in advance and occur on either a weekly or monthly basis.

- Meetings should take place in a comfortable, quiet area of the house and interruptions minimized (i.e. no cell phones).

- All members of the family should be equal participants.

- All members of the family should attend, regardless of age.

- All members of the family should be allowed input into the resolution of issues.

- Consensus should be the preferred approach to decision making.

- Gratitude and appreciation for each other rather than putdowns and disappointments should be encouraged.

ADVANCE NOTICE
Many children have a problem switching from a fun activity such as play to one they perceive to be boring, such as dinner or bedtime. A few minutes before the transition, give your child advance notice. Have him repeat what you have just said so you are clear he understands. When the time comes for the transition, give the command in an assertive but emotionally neutral fashion. Don't engage in an argument if your child protests but, instead, use the punishment-reward system and/or a time out if necessary.

AN UNDERSTANDING TEACHER
Be sure to take extra time and effort in choosing your child's teacher. The compassion, understanding and commitment to the child's well-being that his or her teacher demonstrates can be the single most important variable regarding the success of difficult or temperamental students.

AN ATTITUDE OF GRATITUDE
Children often have a sense of entitlement rather than an attitude of gratitude. Parents promote this disrespectful attitude by not making the child aware of the sacrifices made on their behalf. Parents should let their children know that they often put their children's wants and desires before their own; not to make the child feel guilty but to make them more grateful for what they have.

PATIENCE AND FORGIVENESS

Many difficult children cause conflict with their parents because of their constant need for stimulation. For this reason, it is extremely important to keep cool rather than to invite strife into the home. Similarly, you must constantly remember that you are dealing with a difficult temperament and practice forgiveness each day for your child's behavior, your behavior and any judgments others may have.

TAKE CARE OF YOURSELF
SO YOU CAN TAKE CARE OF YOUR CHILDREN

Parents of difficult children often experience significantly higher levels of stress, depression and self-blame than parents of easier children. You can reduce your level of stress by practicing relaxation techniques, engaging in exercise, pursuing a hobby, listening to music, becoming active in support groups, taking vacations, sharing responsibilities with other parents, and being aware of what you eat and how it affects you. Reread Chapter 3 on Taking Care of Yourself for further suggestions.

Also, children with difficult temperaments have a tendency to interrupt your activities such as when you are talking on the phone, reading or watching television. Explain to your child in a clear, direct manner before you start the activity that you do not want to be interrupted and suggest how your child can stay occupied while you are busy.

Most importantly, give frequent positive feedback when your child demonstrates positive behavior.

DEALING WITH YOUR TEMPERAMENTAL TEEN

Dealing with teenagers can be especially trying for parents even if you are patient and work toward more effective communication. In her book *Why Teens Are So Critical*, Kathleen McCoy, Ph.D., explains that it's perfectly normal for children to become more difficult and temperamental during their teen years and that this phase is just part of the maturation process.

Adolescence generally happens between the ages of eleven and nineteen, during which time your child will undergo several important biological and psychological changes. Throughout this period your child will:

- Mature physically

- Mature sexually

- Define values

- Manifest personal power

- Individuate

He or she will also be dealing with all sorts of new concerns such as physical appearance, the opinions of peers, wanting to belong, drugs and music.

Writes Dr. McCoy: "Your child is working towards one of the major goals of adolescence – learning to be independent. In order to become less dependent, teens need to give new credence to their own ideas and opinions. They need additionally to believe that in separating from you they aren't losing so much. Separating from the person who loves them most would be overwhelming and cause incredible grief, were that person not cut down to very human proportions.

"It can help to understand this process and give teens the freedom to have and voice their own opinions without verbally abusing parents and family. As the teen grows in competence and independence, of course, he or she will feel more secure and able to agree with you on occasion and to admire and accept you in new ways."

Behavior throughout adolescence is guided by the goal of wanting to belong and feeling significant. When kids don't feel this way, they act in a way that seems like misbehavior. However, it is simply a misguided effort to find belonging and significance. This normal aspect of an adolescent's development becomes more problematic for teens who have lost touch with the creative, loving, powerful people they really are. Somewhere along the way they were taught that they were not good enough, not bright enough, not attractive enough, not energetic enough, not strong enough, etc. They took on these negative beliefs about themselves and used them as a foundation for their behavior. In other words, children act out because they have low self-esteem and as a result feel insecure. The following categories describe the ways a teenager (as well as younger children) might try to feel significant and how you, as a parent, can manage their behavior.

DEMANDING UNDUE ATTENTION

The child's mistaken belief is that getting noticed equals being important in your eyes. He or she will try to keep you busy or get your attention for no reason. This desire for attention is often demonstrated when your child interrupts in a conversation you're having with someone in person or on the phone. But the real message is that the child simply wants to be involved. As a parent, rather than feeling annoyed, irritated or guilty, try to really listen and spend quality time with your child.

REBELLION (REFUSAL TO PLAY BY THE RULES)

The need for adolescents to find out who they are by being independent often conflicts with the parent's desire to retain the decision-making authority. When not given input into the decision making process, teens may act out by associating with undesirable friends, doing poorly in academics, abusing drugs and alcohol or breaking rules and boundaries. What is usually behind this behavior is the desire to give feedback and have choices rather than being given orders. Instead of focusing on and punishing them for rebellious behavior, try brainstorming and negotiating as a way of giving them a part in the decision making process. It's an art to do this while making it clear that certain nonnegotiable rules still apply, such as:

- No smoking or drugs

- No cursing in the house

- Telling parents where you are going and what time you will be home

- No friends in the house without parents' permission

GETTING REVENGE

If your child is feeling insignificant or unloved, he or she may strike out by damaging property, being extremely disrespectful or doing something else to get even. Such actions are really a cry for help and an expression of inner hurt. Try not to take the child's behavior personally but, instead, help your child to communicate his or her feelings to you or a professional as a way of processing the hurt.

WITHDRAWAL

Although its outward appearance is very different from the other coping mechanisms, withdrawal, giving up and "caving in" are probably the most painful behavioral qualities for a child to endure. In essence, this child is asking to be respected and treated as worthwhile. Giving this child extra attention, warmth and acknowledgment is the approach that can heal this damaged ego.

We are involved in a more loving, empathetic approach when we focus on our child's insecurity and self-esteem issues and desire to feel significant as causes for misbehavior, rather than on the behavior itself. The following home assignment is intended to demonstrate this understanding at a deeper level.

THE EMPATHY EXERCISE

1. LIST THOSE THINGS THAT WERE IMPORTANT TO YOU AS A
    TEENAGER (E.G. CLOTHES, FRIENDS, PHYSICAL APPEARANCE,
    MUSIC, ETC.)

2. LIST THE VALUES AND SKILLS YOU WANT FOR YOUR
    CHILDREN BY THE TIME THEY ARE 21 YEARS OLD (E.G.
    INDEPENDENCE, HONESTY, SELF-DISCIPLINE, ETC.)

140

3. IMAGINE THIS SCENARIO: YOUR CHILD COMES HOME TWO
    AND A HALF HOURS LATE FROM A PARTY. WRITE DOWN HOW
    YOU WOULD REACT AND WHAT YOU WOULD SAY IN YOUR
    WORST MOMENTS.

4. GO OVER THE LIST OF VALUES AND SKILLS YOU WROTE DOWN
    IN QUESTION #2. DOES YOUR REACTION TO THE SITUATION IN
    QUESTION #3 MODEL BEHAVIOR THAT IS COMPATIBLE WITH
    THESE SAME VALUES AND SKILLS?

11

RESOLVING CONFLICT PEACEFULLY

Instead of me vs. you, we can reframe conflict as a way of working together to bring more wisdom and creativity into the problem-solving process.

Today's youth get involved in more violent confrontations over less serious issues than at any other time in history. Violence permeates talk shows, music, movies, television and music videos at an extraordinary level. By the time the average American child is 16, he or she will view more than 200,000 acts of violence. The media portray violence as glamorous and the preferred way of resolving conflict. As parents, we need to counteract this destructive influence by modeling ways of dealing with conflict situations in a peaceful, constructive and life-affirming way.

HOW YOU RELATE TO THE ISSUE IS THE ISSUE

Before demonstrating peaceful resolution, we need to examine how we relate to the concept of conflict. Frequently, people believe that opposition and the expression of contrary feelings are counterproductive. Nothing could be further from the truth. **Conflict is a necessary, positive and unavoidable part of any relationship.**

Often the first step in identifying and eventually resolving issues is to be in a setting that supports the honest expression of feelings. If discord is repressed and not resolved then resentments build up, feelings get displaced onto others and gossiping and backbiting are encouraged. James Baldwin summed it up when he said, **"Not everything that is faced can be changed but nothing can be changed until it is faced."**

141

SEVEN STEPS TO RESOLVING CONFLICT PEACEFULLY

I.   GET CLEAR ON YOUR INTENTION FOR A PEACEFUL RESOLUTION.
Instead of me vs you, we can reframe conflict as a way of working together to bring more wisdom and intimacy into our relationships. This is quite different from the intention of hurting, attacking, putting down or proving that we are right.

In Chapter 8, I mentioned that before beginning a specific interaction that has the possibility of resulting in disharmony, we should ask ourselves, "Do I want peace or war?" The power of clarifying our intention is exemplified in this personal experience I often share with my high school students:

After two years of research and observation, I finally completed the development of the program that I am currently presenting to students. I had a meeting with a headmaster who had expressed interest in incorporating my program into his school's curriculum. He was quite impressed and we set up a time and agreed on the salary I would be paid for teaching the program. Everything was set and I was to begin my first course in three weeks.

He was not available to talk when I called him a week later to work out a few small details. He didn't call back either. After unsuccessfully trying to reach him several times, I realized that he was not going to honor his agreement. Needless to say, I was very upset. About two months later I saw him walking toward me on the street. I was really angry and my impulse was to verbally unload my hostility on him. As we approached each other I calmed down enough to ask myself, "What is my intention for this interaction? Do I want peace or war?" I chose peace. I began our conversation by telling him in an assertive way that I felt hurt and disappointed. He said that he felt bad but the school psychologist was threatened by my course and he had to make a choice. He apologized and gave me, along with a promise of a personal recommendation, the name of a head master who might be interested. After several meetings, his referral became the first to present my program.

If my intention were war, I probably would have had an argument with the original headmaster and walked away with another enemy in my life. As a result of having the intention for peaceful resolution, I was given the opportunity to present my program for the first time. The power of intention is awesome. We create how our lives look at any particular moment by the choices we make. The clearer we are about our intention before we take action, the more we will experience joy and fulfillment. Nike says, "Just Do It." I say, "Get clear on your intention, then Just Do It."

2. FORGIVE YOURSELF FOR ANY JUDGEMENTS YOU HAVE REGARDING YOUR BEHAVIOR WITH THE OTHER PERSON. This step was exemplified recently after an argument I had with one of my facilitators. I could have called him the next day in order to resolve the residual anger I felt. A week went by and, upon looking deeply, I saw that the reason I hadn't called was that I was ashamed of the anger I displayed during our disagreement. Once I forgave myself (and the judgments I had against myself for displaying anger), I was able to call him and begin the process of reconciliation.

Even if our intention is clear, we can delay the conversation that leads to resolution of a conflict because we have not forgiven the negative judgments we placed against ourselves.

3. FEEL WHAT YOU ARE FEELING WITH NONJUDGMENTAL AWARENESS. This begins by feeling the specific physical sensations in our body. This process can be assisted by closing our eyes, which makes it easier to go inside.

Explorers of the human psyche such as Gay Hendrix, Elizabeth Haye and Oscar Ichazo, among others, have investigated how specific emotions affect the functioning of different parts of the body. For instance, the jaws register anger, the throat and chest register loss and sadness, the stomach registers fear and the genitals register guilt. Focusing on the discomfort in our bodies assists us in identifying our present emotions as well as producing relevant images from our past that may be contributing to our present state. **Feelings are valuable in that they tell us what is true for us in the moment. Accessing them allows our intuition to guide us toward our next step.**

Instead of observing our bodies and emotions, we often go into our heads and try to figure things out. Thinking and rationalizing instead of feeling and sensing are ways of attempting to control our reality. It seems as if we spend a lot of our lives controlling, pretending and defending ourselves instead of being vulnerable and just feeling what we're feeling.

Even when we do feel, we have been taught which emotions are acceptable and which are not. Beliefs such as, "A decent person doesn't feel anger," "Feeling sexually attracted to someone is bad," "Men don't cry," and "Fear is bad" have greatly impaired our emotional expression. **Pain enters our lives every time there is a distance between how we really feel and how we think we are supposed to feel.** You get angry and instead of letting that feeling in and feeling it for a few seconds you rationalize, "I shouldn't be angry" or "It's really nothing." You see someone you're attracted to and instead of acting on that feeling you find a reason not to like them.

Feelings can never be denied or fixed, they just need to be acknowledged, experienced and observed. Instead of just experiencing feelings, we often turn to trying to control others, co-dependency and perfectionism. Food, alcohol and drug addictions are strategies also used in order not to feel what is going on inside ourselves. **A harmonious flow begins when we are able to sit with and accept, rather than intellectualize, suppress or deny what we are feeling.**

4. TAKE RESPONSIBILITY FOR YOUR FEELINGS AND YOUR PART IN THE CONFLICT. There is always the tendency to want to blame others. As we discussed in Chapter 7, Forgiveness, when we blame others we get to be right, justify our anger and not take responsibility for our part in the situation. We also get no true resolution. For there to be any possibility of resolving conflict peacefully, we must acknowledge our part in creating, promoting or allowing the conflict.

We next take responsibility for being the source of our anger. Again, **nobody else makes us angry; we choose to get upset over someone else's behavior.**

5. COMMUNICATE THE FUNDAMENTAL TRUTH OF WHAT YOU ARE FEELING. Communicating your feelings produces a different result than telling your child their behavior is unacceptable. For example, "I feel upset and taken advantage of when I see the mess in your room an hour after I've cleaned" is different from, "You're old enough to keep your room clean." The first is an "I" statement in which you take responsibility for how you feel. The second is a "you" statement which alienates your child by criticizing his or her actions.

It can be short and honest with no blame intended. "I" statements, such as: "I've been thinking about ending this relationship," "I feel treated unfairly," "I feel hurt," "I feel unloved," and "I feel you don't respect me," are statements of truth and demonstrate a willingness to take responsibility rather than blame the other person.

Problems in relationships are more often caused by what we don't say rather than by what we do say. In order to relate openly, we have to be willing to be intimate with ourselves and others. True intimacy begins by communicating our truth in the moment.

145

What often prevents us from communicating our inner truth can be traced back to childhood. At a point in our development we were made to feel that because of the behavior we were demonstrating, we were inadequate. Wanting to be loved, we developed a persona, an act that would guarantee that people would accept us. It becomes very difficult to communicate what is true for us in the moment when what we feel conflicts with this persona. For example, a three-year-old's parents didn't like it when she was disruptive and difficult. As a consequence, she learned to be a "good" girl so her parents would like her. After years this persona has become so ingrained that she no longer sees it as an act but, instead, as who she really is.

Now she is 34 and in a relationship. When she gets angry, instead of communicating her anger, she has learned to be a "nice person" and nice people don't get angry. She is hindered in intimacy because she thinks that her boyfriend will not like her if she shows him the part that she hides.

Although we have adopted different characters, this scenario is being played out in all of our lives. Some of us have become the "angry person" who was made to feel wrong as a child for showing his sensitivity. Or the "aloof person" who was chastised for being too attached and needy. Or the "clown" who couldn't get attention by being serious or real. Have you become the "intellectual" because you were rewarded with love for being so smart? Or are you the "rebel" who couldn't get enough attention by being good?

The next exercise will make us more aware of the habitual roles we play when conflict arises by defining our behavior in terms of what animal we most resemble.

YOU'RE SUCH AN ANIMAL EXERCISE

A. Which animal most represents your style when conflict arises?

1. **SHEEP...** "Whatever you say is fine"
    Advantage: You are sensitive to others feelings and keep the peace in order to maintain relationships.
    Disadvantage: Your needs are rarely met. You are left with anger and resentment.

2. **OSTRICH...** "Leave me alone – I have nothing to do with it"
    Advantage: You never get into a fight
    Disadvantage: You feel powerless because you have no input into what goes on in your life.

3. **SHARK.** "My way or the highway"
    Advantage: You are always willing to speak up, take charge and take risks.
    Disadvantage: You rarely really listen to others' point of view. Winning is more important than relationship.

4. **OWL...** "Let's work it out together"
   Advantage: You respect others' point of view, and look for accommodation and compromise. You create trust and build relationships.
   Disadvantage: It's not easy being an owl. It takes commitment and courage.

B. **Why do you think you chose the role you chose?** For example, "I became a sheep as a teenager because my parents gave me things when I didn't say anything and just went along with what they thought was right for me." Or, "I became a shark, because my father was a shark and the only way he would listen is if I yelled louder than he did."

C. **In another time in your life did your style resemble a different animal than it does now?**

D. **Which animal do you want to be like? What prevents you from being more like that animal?**

In fact who we really are is none of these characters. Who we really are can't be defined because it is changing from moment to moment. It is our fixed persona that prevents us from responding genuinely to each moment.

---

6. LISTEN SO YOU CAN ACKNOWLEDGE AND RESPECT THE OTHER PERSON'S PERSPECTIVE. For there to be peaceful resolution, we must be able to not only acknowledge that the other person has a point of view, but also to understand **that their way of perceiving the situation is as valid to them as our interpretation is to us.** In order to understand the other person's point of view, we must be able to listen. Once we do that, we can recognize the other person's needs, desires, priorities and values. As we discovered in the chapter on emotion coaching, the ability to empathize is a very important step in the process.

7. LOOK FOR A SOLUTION WHERE BOTH PARTIES WIN. This is difficult, but the intention for peace can evoke creative solutions to most problems. When parent and child utilize a consensus approach, no force is required in implementing the solution since the decision was mutually agreed upon. On the other hand, when the parent dictates and the child has no input in the decision-making process:

148

- The parent communicates that the child in not sensitive, resourceful or mature enough to find a solution.

- Children typically resist being told what to do.

- Since the child has no investment in the decision they have very little motivation to carry it out.

Consensus, which utilized the wisdom of the parent as well as the child, is applicable to common family areas of contention such as delegation of chores, allowances, use of a computer, television watching, use of a phone, condition of rooms, appropriate bedtime, etc.

First, identify the conflict, then generate and evaluate alternative solutions and finally find a solution that both parent and child can "live with". "Live with" does not mean "love" or "prefer", it means finding a solution that all involved are "willing to support".

NOBODY EVER SAID IT WAS EASY

Even if our intention for peaceful resolution is clear and we have promised ourselves that we will never yell again, the reality is that we sometimes let ourselves down. Just as in our approach to forgiveness, the acknowledgment and expression of anger is often a necessary step on the way to resolving conflict. In this chapter, the preferred path to peaceful resolution has been presented. It is an alternative and often very difficult approach for those of you who habitually attempt to resolve conflict by the verbal or physical expression of anger. It is not easy to change habitual patterns. Again, acceptance and being gentle with ourselves is the most nurturing approach.

One more comment: Concise steps and numbered categories are often used in personal growth books and articles as a way of simplifying the process of dealing with life and its challenges. This approach seems to satisfy that lazy part of us that wants clear-cut explanations without having to go through the effort of creative exploration. The steps presented in this chapter provide information and a framework for effectively dealing with emotional issues. They are not a magic bullet that, when employed, will work correctly in every conflict situation. When we have internalized the understanding, empathy and communication skills that are necessary for peaceful resolution, we will spontaneously know how to respond when conflict arises.

149

RESOLVING CONFLICT PEACEFULLY

There are seven principles that foster the peaceful resolution of a conflict situation:

1. HAVING THE INTENTION FOR PEACEFUL RESOLUTION
2. FORGIVE OURSELF FOR ANY JUDGEMENTS WE HAVE REGARDING OUR BEHAVIOR WITH THE OTHER PERSON
3. FEELING OUR FEELINGS
4. TAKING RESPONSIBILITY FOR OUR PART IN THE CONFLICT
5. COMMUNICATING OUR FEELINGS
6. HAVING EMPATHY FOR THE OTHER PERSON'S POINT OF VIEW
7. FINDING A SOLUTION WHERE BOTH PEOPLE WIN

150

REFLECT ON A RECENT ARGUMENT OR CURRENT DISAGREEMENT YOU ARE HAVING WITH ANOTHER PERSON. DESCRIBE THE SPECIFICS OF THE CONFLICT AND WRITE ABOUT HOW YOU USED EACH OF THE ABOVE PRINCIPLES TO RESOLVE THIS CONFLICT.

PARTICIPANTS' COMMENTS

- In writing about her experience with a difficult student and the power of intention in resolving conflict, a teacher noted, "Besides being unruly, he usually was unprepared. I've publicly chided him in front of the class for his tardiness, lack of preparedness and poor academic production. That only seemed to make matters worse. I decided to change my approach.

    When I saw him in the hall during passing period I said, 'Good morning,' and told him that I hope to see him in class early – prepared to participate with the rest of his peers. Since doing this, his attitude and performance have changed. He needed to be disciplined in a sincere, loving manner in order for positive change to take place."

- After observing her passive communication pattern for a week, a teacher shared:

    "I noticed that I need to impress people or make people happy even at the expense of my own happiness. A lot of the things that I did this week had to do with me thinking that I had to make sure I did not put anyone in an uncomfortable situation, regardless of whether or not I was happy. I didn't want to bring people down, make people think less of me or disappoint anyone."

    This behavior is called worshipping the God of another's opinion.

- Another teacher shared:

    "My principal called me and somewhere in the conversation began to berate my colleague for an incident. He seemed to fault her for everything that was wrong with the world. Here's where I challenged my usual 'anything is better than conflict' approach. I decided that I would speak my mind. I let him know that I did not agree with him.

The principal seemed to respect that I had the courage to question his opinion and that I felt at peace with myself."

12

IRRATIONAL BELIEFS AND DESTRUCTIVE HABITS

Becoming masterful parents requires identifying and changing the irrational beliefs that influence our perceptions of ourselves, others and the world.

When we were very young, we viewed reality in innocence. We experienced each moment as fresh and new, and had very few beliefs about the world to color what we saw. As adults, however, we have acquired all sorts of beliefs about ourselves, others and the world. Even if these beliefs are hidden, they cloud our perception and as a result influence our behavior.

On closer examination, we find that many of these beliefs are contradictory, based on single instances that we have unwisely turned into generalizations. The psychologist Albert Ellis calls these "irrational beliefs". For example, some of us carry in our minds the idea that overweight people are lazy, unhealthy, and sad; however, we also think of this group as "jolly". Clearly, both of these generalizations cannot be true. In fact, neither of them is. Until we examine such hidden irrational beliefs, they remain uncontested and continue influence our perceptions and actions.

Irrational beliefs are the basis for all stereotypes. When we assume an attitude toward someone we are meeting for the first time, we are responding to a stereotype we carry within us. "You are Jewish, therefore...," "You are black, therefore...," "You are a woman, therefore...," "You are rich/poor/old/fat...." You name it, if there's a stereotype, then there's also an irrational belief to match.

Rational beliefs, on the other hand, are beliefs based on unwavering facts. They can be proven true in every case. I believe, for example, that if I let go of my pen, it will drop to the floor. I can test this and prove it by getting the same result every time. Irrational beliefs, however, do not stand up to the test of what is true in reality.

As we've discussed throughout this book, many of our beliefs come from the past. If I was once bitten by a dog, I may see all dogs, even the gentlest of pups, as vicious and dangerous. Some irrational beliefs are simply prejudices we have acquired from our parents or the communities in which we were raised. Beliefs like "All rich people get their money by lying and cheating," or "Poor people are too lazy to work and make money," or "Crying is a sign of weakness," are irrational because they cannot be consistently shown to be true.

IRRATIONAL BELIEFS ABOUT OURSELVES AS INDIVIDUALS

Irrational beliefs not only influence the way we view others but also distort the way we see ourselves. Let's discuss a few of these irrational beliefs about ourselves:

I LOSE MY POWER IF I ALLOW MYSELF TO BE VULNERABLE.

Many of us struggle or have struggled with this one. The reason is plain to see: all of us, at one time or another, have been hurt by someone who took advantage of our vulnerability. On some level we were all betrayed by parents who could never match the love we had for them when we were young. Maybe it was another family member, partner, friend or the schoolyard bully whom we felt betrayed us. Nevertheless, it is irrational to believe that being vulnerable always results in pain and loss of power. **Allowing ourselves to be vulnerable, especially in intimate relationships, is necessary to establish the trust that makes love possible.**

Adopting the above irrational belief is a way of eliminating from our lives the pain caused by relationships. Similarly irrational beliefs such as: "Men can't be trusted," "I have lost the only person I could ever love," "Men are incapable of making commitments," "Because I couldn't trust my parents, I can't trust anyone else," "Relationships are just about suffering, so why bother?" are often manifestations of our fears. These beliefs may serve the function of protecting us from the reoccurrence of past hurts but the price we pay is often decreased vitality, isolation and a lost opportunity to experience the joy and lessons learned from being intimate with another person.

I SHOULD FEEL BAD FOR A LONG TIME AFTER I DO SOMETHING WRONG.

This is an irrational belief that causes many of us a great deal of unnecessary suffering. This particular belief is rooted in superstition: if I make myself feel bad enough for long enough, then the heavens, or God, or fate, will have mercy on me and not punish me too badly. This belief usually comes from childhood experience when "the heavens" meant our parents or other adults in authority. Perhaps they even abused that authority by supporting this belief. In any case, what possible good can come from feeling bad for a long time? Guilt only produces resentment toward ourselves and others. Looking at mistakes as an opportunity to learn rather than as a time to beat ourselves up seems to be a more rational approach.

Almost any belief about ourselves that begins with "I should" is irrational. We need to meet and accept ourselves where we are. Otherwise we hurt ourselves by applying stereotypes to ourselves. Here are just a few of the many irrational beliefs we have about ourselves that cause confusion and suffering:

- Because I have failed at _____ , I am a worthless person.

- Other people cause me to be angry.

- A man should deal with his problems on his own.

- Being able to take pain makes me more manly.

- When people act unfairly, I should blame them and see them as wicked individuals.

- Emotional misery comes from outside of me.

- Women should never show anger.

- If something seems frightening, I have no choice but to preoccupy myself with worrying about it.

- Life would be easy if I had money.

- If I don't fight back, I'm a wimp.

- I should be nice to everyone.

- I should be thinner.

IRRATIONAL BELIEFS ABOUT OTHER PEOPLE

Irrational beliefs about others not only hurt them but also ourselves, because we are weakened whenever we disengage and take our hearts away. The "shoulds" we inflict on others also keep us from seeing who people really are. Here are a couple of examples:

OLD PEOPLE ARE WISE.

This is a stereotype. This particular irrational belief, common in our culture, may seem positive on the surface. (Certainly it's better than, "old people are stupid.") However, it still takes the irrational step of identifying a person's status (wise) with a category (old people). In working with both parents and children, I have found many youngsters who were much wiser than their parents. If people became wiser as they grew older then the world, by now, would be a peaceful and prosperous paradise, wouldn't it?

Irrational beliefs that create expectations can place unreasonable demands on people. The idea that all blacks are good athletes, all Chinese are mathematical geniuses or all Italians are great cooks conceivably places a great deal of pressure on any member of these groups. All of these ideas have power over us when they are hidden but don't hold up when we stop and examine them.

KIDS TODAY ARE ROTTEN.

This belief comes from newspapers, television and films. Sadly, we find few positive portraits of teens in the media. Remember that there is a simple scientific test for a rational belief (like letting go of the pen and watching it drop to the floor) – it must be able to be tested and proven true in every case. Clearly, using this guideline, the statement that "kids today are rotten" is an irrational belief. Besides, if you stop to think about it, adults have always been saying this about "kids today". This next quote exemplifies just how long adults have been complaining about kids.

> "The children now love luxury; they have bad manners;
> contempt for authority; show disrespect for elders...
> Children are now tyrants, not the servants of their households...
> They contradict their parents...and tyrannize their teachers."
>
> Socrates, c. 390 B.C.

It's easy to acquire a head full of irrational beliefs about other people. Prejudices and stereotypes are always readily available. Here are some other irrational beliefs about other people. How many of them do you recognize, at least sometimes, as your own?

- People should turn out better than they do.

- Women should marry by 30.

- This is the way teenagers are and they'll probably never change.

- Teenagers don't really know what's best for themselves.

- People who work with their hands are not as smart as people who work in offices.

- People who smoke are too weak to quit.

- People who go to church are good; people who don't are bad.

- New Yorkers are cold and unfriendly.

- Lawyers are crooks.

- White southerners are racists.

- Men are insensitive.

- People who are overweight don't have willpower.

- Rich people are arrogant.

IRRATIONAL BELIEFS ABOUT RELATIONSHIPS

Along with our irrational beliefs about ourselves and others, most of us find that we have quite a few irrational beliefs about relationships as well. For example:

IF YOU LOVE SOMEONE, THEN YOU DON'T FIGHT AND ARGUE WITH THEM.

It is my experience that the exact opposite belief is more often true: The people we love are the people we tend to argue with the most. As stated previously, the ones we love hurt us the most deeply and as a result most often trigger emotional reactions. This is because intimate relationships provide us with the opportunity to heal that part of ourselves that was damaged at an earlier stage of development. Part of this healing process is the triggering of past emotions that were never completely resolved. According to Harville Hendrix, **the function of love is to bring up and heal everything that is not love.** By viewing this as one of the main functions of a relationship, we make room for the discord that occurs in every intimate relationship.

Think about it: arguing and trying to persuade someone else of your point of view are ways of saying, "I care about what you think." After all, if you didn't, you would simply walk away, wouldn't you? The truth is that successful couples find ways to argue that do not violate each other's dignity and do not damage the relationship.

A PERSON WHO REALLY LOVES ME WOULD KNOW HOW I FEEL AND WHAT I NEED WITHOUT MY HAVING TO TELL THEM.

This particular irrational belief may be the single biggest producer of

158

pain and sadness in relationships. It is a combination of fairytale romance and a superstitious view of love as something that is "true" or not, instead of something two people create and nurture together. Even the most compatible people cannot always know what each other is thinking. Empathy is not mind-reading. This irrational belief is a totally useless excuse for poor communication. Let me offer you a rational belief to replace it: **Relationships are nurtured when people clearly communicate their needs, feelings and desires.**

Irrational beliefs about relationships are especially painful because they tend to negatively affect both parties. Nobody comes out unhurt when these beliefs are operating. Let's look at a few others. Recognize any of them?

- If you hurt me, I have no choice but to hurt you back.

- It is bad to be jealous.

- People have to earn my forgiveness.

- If I close my heart, it will hurt the other person, and I will win.

- When a relationship ends, the person who leaves first is the winner.

- When a relationship starts to feel routine, it's over.

- When I do something nice for someone, they should return the favor.

- I never will make it longer than a year in a relationship.

- Relationships are made in heaven.

- If this relationship doesn't work out, I'll never find anyone else.

- If I ever left him, he couldn't go on without me.

- You should always feel passion toward the one you love.

159

IRRATIONAL BELIEFS ABOUT PARENTS AND CHILDREN

Since we are talking about becoming masterful parents, let's look at some commonly held, often hidden, irrational beliefs about parents and children, and especially about the relationships between parents and adolescents. You will find a lot of "shoulds" in here – a tip-off that we have left the world of rational expectations behind and entered the "Twilight Zone" of irrational beliefs.

I AM NOT A GOOD PARENT UNLESS I GIVE MY CHILDREN EVERYTHING THEY WANT.

Hardly any of us would actually agree with this statement but remember that most irrational beliefs are hidden; they operate below the level of awareness. This is one of the harder ones to change because we are swimming against the tide of our consumer culture which sends us this message every day through television, radio, magazines and movies. Our kids also get their daily dose of this toxic message. It is, after all, the job of advertisers to get kids to want things and to get you to feel guilty enough to pay for those things. If we examine this irrational belief, we see that, of course, giving our children whatever they want does not make us good parents.

Sadly, I have known several children from extremely wealthy households who got everything they ever asked for. However, they didn't get the things that count for a great deal more: guidance, support, examples of good judgment and a sense of balance in their lives.

On the other side, I have had economically less fortunate parents say: "I resented my parents for giving me very little materially when I was growing up, so I am trying to give my children everything they want." These are the same parents who often speak about not having enough money to buy nice things for themselves. Kids are very smart and can be extremely manipulative. I have seen them become extremely spoiled and demanding using this attitude to their advantage. It is my observation that giving based on past disappointment and guilt does not serve us or our children.

IF I DO AND SAY ALL THE RIGHT THINGS, MY CHILDREN WILL COMMUNICATE WITH ME OPENLY AND HONESTLY.

This is another irrational belief not worth the suffering it causes. It is a reflection of the equally irrational belief that our children are merely reflections of ourselves. Children are people, not products. When we model good communication for our children, we do it because it is right, because we love them and because they need that demonstration. We cannot expect them to always follow our lead. **We need to respect the fact that our children have their own process** and identity, and it is important to allow them to be vague or remain silent when they feel it is appropriate.

PARENTS SHOULD NEVER APOLOGIZE TO THEIR CHILDREN.

This irrational belief stems from the feeling that parents must always maintain the upper hand. Perhaps this belief came from our families or our culture but like all other irrational beliefs, it falls flat in the face of reason. This is real life not an imaginary world where parents are always kind, gentle, understanding, patient and right. We are people. People make mistakes. That's why pencils have erasers and people have apologies. We need to develop the humility and honesty that make us able to apologize to our children when we have behaved in a manner that does not serve them. This vulnerability creates intimacy and trust and demonstrates a deep level of integrity.

161

Although we have acquired many irrational beliefs, it seems as if we become even more susceptible to their influence when we become parents. We want so much to be good parents. We want so much for our children. We expect a great deal from ourselves and our kids. There's nothing wrong with high standards but as we have seen, irrational beliefs are something different – they do nothing to improve our lives or the lives of our children. Instead, they undermine us, frustrate our intentions and rob us of the joy that can be ours.

I JUDGE MY SUCCESS AS A PARENT BY HOW WELL MY CHILD LOOKS, DRESSES, SOCIALIZES AND WHAT THEY ACHIEVE.

"Producing" a child who is "extremely bright", "gifted", "polite" and/or "a great athlete" has become a status symbol for many parents. Often, these parents are unfulfilled in their own lives, and use their children as a source of self-worth and self-esteem. In many cases, they look to their child for the satisfaction and pleasure lacking in their relationship with their spouse, or as a substitute for intimate adult relationships. These circumstances often produce an overprotective, critical environment where the child is unduly pressured academically and socially.

In many cases, "producing" a "special" son or daughter is more attractive and less difficult than maintaining an intimate, loving adult relationship. A spouse often runs a distant second to the child for attention and nurturing. However, nothing has a greater impact on the social and emotional well-being of a child than the quality of relationship of the adults they observe day in and day out – their parents.

There are a number of single parents participating in our programs that have not healed their own wounds. They are motivated to "produce" overly independent children who will avoid the pain of being dependent on another person (spouse) for fulfillment. There is nothing wrong with having children develop into independent, free-thinking adults; but the outcomes are quite different when the message is driven by unresolved anger, non-forgiveness and hurt rather than what is best for the child.

Other irrational beliefs parents harbor are:

- Parents should be perfect.

- It's my job to keep my child from experiencing pain and failure.

- Parents are the only key to a child's success.

- Obedience is more important than having a child think, be responsible, and learn from his or her mistakes.

- My child lives in my house, I pay for everything, so he must listen, do his chores and spend his money exactly how I want him to.

- I know what my children really need, so I'm the best one to plan activities for them.

- I shouldn't have to tell my spouse or child to do things.... They should know what has to be done and just do it.

- A good parent never loses patience with his or her children.

- Parents always know what is best for their children.

- A teenager doesn't really know what's best for him or her.

- (For single parents): My child would do much better if his father/ mother were around.

- I shouldn't have been so lenient when my child was little.

- I know best whom my child should be friends with.

- I am a failure because I got divorced.

IRRATIONAL BELIEFS EXERCISE

1. WRITE DOWN YOUR NEXT BIG GOAL.

2. WRITE DOWN A LIST OF ALL THE POSITIVE BELIEFS AND A LIST OF ALL THE NEGATIVE BELIEFS ASSOCIATED WITH THE ACCOMPLISHMENT OF YOUR GOAL.

3. ARE THERE ANY IRRATIONAL BELIEFS OPERATING THAT COULD BE AFFECTING THE ACCOMPLISHMENT OF YOUR GOAL?

DESTRUCTIVE HABITS

Like irrational beliefs, many habits have been passed down to us by others. For instance, we learned to relate in a certain way by observing our parents communicating with each other. The manner in which we organize our homes has been greatly influenced by the environment we were brought up in. Or we may have become teenage smokers as a result of observing older people smoke. Interestingly, there are also instances where people have cultivated traits that are the opposite of what they observed or were taught at an early age. For example, there are men and women who have developed a very aggressive mode of expression because they do not want to be like their passive fathers or mothers.

Remember the exercise in the *Acceptance* homework that dealt with accepting our every thought, feeling and action in each moment? **There are certain destructive habits that we have developed as a way of coping with thoughts, feelings and actions that we are unable to accept and unwilling to experience.** Habitually having a "social" drink because of not wanting to accept the uncomfortable feeling of meeting a new person, eating sweets instead of accepting a feeling of sadness or overworking as a way of avoiding what is going on in our life emotionally are all ways of avoiding our feelings.

AWARENESS COUNTS

For change to occur, we must first have awareness. For example, we became better listeners when we became aware of what we did instead of listening. We communicated more effectively when we became aware of the habitual patterns of communication that were not serving us.

Likewise, an important step in transforming habits that do not serve us is to take them from the domain of habits into the light of awareness. We do this by asking ourselves in each moment, why we are doing what we are doing. For example, instead of habitually lighting a cigarette ask yourself, "Why am I lighting this cigarette?" "What feelings am I having that I'm unwilling to accept or experience?" This challenge can be used for any habit: "Why am I eating now when I'm not even hungry?" "Why am I sitting here staring at the TV when I have so much work to do?" "Why am I talking about this person behind their back?"

The best time to ask these questions and challenge the fixation is before you light the next cigarette, eat the next Twinkie, worry or yell. The most effective time to break the habitual pattern is at the beginning of the cycle; not the end.

Questioning behavior that does not serve us brings it into our conscious awareness and is a key step in the process towards change.

ANOTHER MENTION OF INTENTION

Once again the importance of the power of intention comes into play. It is obvious that change does not occur until we first have the intention to change. For most people it seems natural to follow the intention to change with an effort to eliminate the specific habit. This is a great idea, except that it usually doesn't work. How many times have you failed at quitting smoking, overeating, rushing, uncontrollable anger, lateness, etc.?

Our chances for success are significantly increased when we ask ourselves: "What is my intention regarding this area of my life"? For instance: "I want to be more vital and have more socializing in my life." This is a different starting point than "I want to lose weight". "I want to be able to breathe easily, feel healthier and not always be coughing" is different from "I want to stop smoking". The intention of wanting a more loving and peaceful relationship with your wife has more power than "I want to stop yelling and screaming".

Up to now, many of you have been trying the elimination approach. See if it works better to instead focus on a positive intention for a specific area of your life.

One final observation about the nature of intention and our power as creators: **The universe supports us so completely that sometimes, when we get clear on what we want and if it's for our highest good, it will be given to us just because we have asked for it.**

DO YOU DESERVE WHAT YOU ARE ASKING FOR?

You may be jumping up and down with the realization that the game is finally over now that you have understood that all there is to do for change to occur is to be aware of the consequences of a specific habit and have the intention for positive change. I hate to burst your bubble but we've only just begun.

Earlier we mentioned that, "nobody is going to give you what you don't think you deserve." **The intentions we have for ourselves reflect what we think we deserve.** We can apply this concept by looking at and possibly upgrading our intention for specific areas of our lives.

Are you living at the material level you would like? What do you feel you deserve regarding material well being? What beliefs have prevented you from setting your intentions higher? Are you willing to upgrade your intention?

Regarding your health and physical appearance, are you functioning at optimum health? Do you feel comfortable at your present weight? Are you willing to upgrade your intention regarding your physical appearance?

Regarding your primary relationship, what is your intention for the future growth and expansion of the relationship? Are you willing to upgrade your intention? If you are not presently involved in a relationship, what qualities do you think you deserve in your next one?

We can have awareness and intention, but the life transformation that occurs through changing destructive habits may not occur until we are willing to look at the source of our beliefs concerning our capacity and our right to manifest our full potential at every level. There are several deep-seated irrational beliefs that we may have acquired somewhere along the way that can be subtly influencing our ability to manifest our desires:

- GOD IS AGAINST ME

- I AM NOT WORTHY OF SUCCESS

- IF I HAVE THIS MUCH FEAR OR ANGER INSIDE OF ME THEN I DON'T DESERVE ANY TYPE OF REWARD

Before I started observing them, these irrational beliefs were operating at an unconscious level to undermine fulfillment and positive change in my life. For example, I would get angry when there was a lightning storm and my phone would not work. Being aware that we get angry because life doesn't show up the way we think it "should" is one level of understanding. At a deeper level, I began to see that underneath my anger was the belief that God was making my life difficult because he didn't like me. More often than not, recalling this understanding when the opportunity for upset occurs, dissipates the anger and produces a calmer response.

Again, there are times when I am not proud of my emotional response to a situation. After an outburst I sometimes think "How can I teach others social and emotional skills if I can't control my own emotions?" This is irrational and destructive thinking. If we had to wait until we were perfect to teach anything, nothing would ever get taught.

Another area where the issue of worthiness comes into play is when we have to decide whether we deserve to buy something for ourselves. Have you ever seen an item of clothing that you liked and could afford to buy but didn't? What was keeping you from making that purchase? Very often it's the feeling that you don't deserve it. I equate self-worth with self-nurturing. This refers to Chapter 3 where we spoke about the importance of taking care of ourselves physically, emotionally, mentally and spiritually.

Throughout this book I have been asking you to consider choices that will nurture you in every area of your life. Forgiving ourselves and others, taking responsibility for creating what occurs in our lives, accepting ourselves and others and speaking our truth in a considerate manner are all ways of nurturing ourselves. The question is: **"Do we love ourselves enough to do what is best for ourselves in every moment?"**

Once we become aware of a habit we may never have thought about before (for example, learning that it doesn't serve us to indulge the negative voice inside of ourselves), we then have the choice to change. What is it that could allow this habit to continue, even though we now know that it doesn't serve us and that a better choice is available? First of all, it is the nature of a habit to continually repeat itself. We can't stop our negative self-talk from appearing; but what we can do, once it begins, is not feed it. How long are you willing to allow this negative talk to continue inside of you? Is it five seconds, five minutes, five hours, five days? This is where choice and willpower come into play. It is my experience that how long I am willing to let negativity continue once it has begun has to do with how willing I am to nurture myself. This applies not only to negative self-talk, but also to habits such as negatively judging others, overeating, impatience, procrastination, etc. Think about it – at every moment are you your own best friend? **At every moment are you doing whatever it takes to nurture yourself?** If not... then why not?

Maybe our parents, society, a teacher, a sibling or a peer told us we were not good enough. Maybe all of them did. After many generations, maybe we were born with a feeling of lack. I am not exactly sure how negative beliefs about our self-worth became so deeply imbedded in our consciousness, but I do know that they are there and that these beliefs don't serve us in becoming fulfilled human beings. Let me reinforce this point by reiterating Nelson Mandela's 1994 Inaugural Address where he quoted Marianne Williamson:

169

"Our worst fear is not that we are inadequate. Our deepest fear is that we are powerful beyond measure. It is our light not our darkness that most frightens us. We ask ourselves who am I to be brilliant, gorgeous, talented and fabulous. Actually, who are you not to be? You are a child of God. Your playing small doesn't serve the world. There is nothing enlightened about shrinking so that others don't feel insecure around you. We were born to make manifest the glory of God within us. It is in everyone and as we let our own light shine we unconsciously give other people permission to do the same. As we are liberated from our fear our presence automatically liberates others."

DESTRUCTIVE HABITS

FROM THE FOLLOWING LIST, PICK ONE DESTRUCTIVE HABIT YOU WOULD LIKE TO CHANGE. THEN ASK YOURSELF AND RECORD:

1. WHY DO I DO IT AND HOW DOES IT AFFECT ME?

2. WHAT IS MY POSITIVE INTENTION FOR THIS PART OF MY LIFE? WHAT DO I DESERVE?

170

3. WHAT CAN I DO DIFFERENTLY?

4. WHAT HAPPENS WHEN I DO IT DIFFERENTLY?

We have been practicing some of these destructive habits for years, perhaps for most of our lives. Again, be patient and loving towards yourself. Personal transformation isn't easy nor does it happen overnight.

LIST OF DESTRUCTIVE HABITS

- Putting things off (procrastinating)
- Working too hard or not working hard enough
- Ignoring problems
- Arguing
- Starting things and not finishing them
- Over-sleeping or not getting enough sleep
- Abusing sugar
- Talking about others behind their backs
- Making excuses and blaming others
- Not saying what you really want to say
- Over-eating or not eating enough
- Being disorganized or being too organized
- Not telling the truth
- Worrying
- Gossiping
- Making fun of others
- Saying "yes" when you want to say "no"
- Always rushing and being late
- Not listening
- Interrupting others when they're talking
- Watching TV
- Letting your jealousy, envy, anger or other emotions run you
- Wasting time
- Giving advice that isn't asked for
- Spending more money than you earn
- Talking too much
- Being a chronic complainer
- Abusing drugs, tobacco or alcohol
- Forgetting names or other important things
- Being over critical of others
- Not taking care of details
- Losing things

PARTICIPANTS' COMMENTS

- A father shared that no matter what he did, his 16-year-old son would not talk to him. He mentioned how his neighbor and his neighbor's son always talked and had a good time together. He said he was even trying to tape messages for his son. He had tried almost everything in an effort to communicate. I pointed out a couple irrational beliefs that he was demonstrating:

  If my kid doesn't talk to me, it's because I've failed as a parent.

  I pay for my son's clothes, rent, transportation, food, etc. The least he could do is talk to me.

  Our discussion brought up the following questions: "Did you ever just accept your son's behavior regarding his communication with you? Did you ever consider that your son's desire not to communicate with you has nothing to do with you? Maybe you shouldn't take his behavior personally." The father said he'd never considered these possibilities. Like a lot of males he was very action oriented and just wanted to fix the problem. I also pointed out that teenagers go through a tough process. They are at an age when they feel a pressing need to separate from their parents in order to establish their own identities. Yet they rely on their parents for food, shelter and clothing. Not communicating can be a way to have some control in an environment where they have very little control.

- A woman confided that she felt like a failure and was very unsure of herself regarding her parenting skills because her 22-year-old son was serving time in jail for attempted robbery. We discussed her irrational beliefs such as:

  If I'd been a good parent my child would never have gone to jail.

  It's my job as a parent to keep my child from experiencing pain.

  My value as a human being is determined by how my child turns out.

Along with these observations the class had incredible empathy for her process.

- A drug counselor shared that he felt like a failure each time one of his patients went back to drugs. This was an example of the irrational belief: "If my patient fails, it's my fault." We can do the best we can to be of service but in the end people are responsible for their own evolution.

- A teacher in my course spoke about how upset she would get when she couldn't "reach" a student. Again, the irrational belief: "It's my fault if a student doesn't respond." My position as a teacher is that I try as hard as I can to reach each student. The reality is that not every student is ready to hear what I have to teach. Not only is this my experience as a teacher but as a student I have not always been ready to hear what was being presented.

173

- A male teacher once told me, "When I go to the movies and I see a man cry, it really makes me sick. I want to throw up." He went on to explain, "When my father died, my three brothers and I were standing around the casket checking each other out to make sure none of us cried."

  This man was a wonderful teacher who was only beginning to see that some of his beliefs were irrational and a product of cultural crosswiring.

- Another teacher said she wanted to figure out how she could live more efficiently so she wouldn't be rushing so much. What I noticed while she was speaking about her pattern of rushing was that she didn't seem to enjoy what she was doing while she was doing it. Her enjoyment seemed to come from checking items off her "to do" list.

  Gradually, it became evident that her lesson was more about enjoying what she was doing as she was doing it rather than doing less. Dislodging the irrational belief that fueled her habit of rushing, the belief that she would be happier if she were able to check more things off on her list, was the key that opened the door of change.

- A parent, who had too much to do and not enough time in the day to finish it all, dealt with her destructive habit of not getting enough sleep by allocating more responsibilities to her children. "Instead of checking their homework I trusted that they were doing a good job. Instead of me, I had them wash their own clothes and do the dishes. I paid them for doing these chores, so it became a win-win situation."

- Another teacher, while focusing on her destructive habit of doing things at the last minute, realized that although this habit produced stress – she actually enjoyed, and functioned very effectively, under pressure. She realized that her habit of waiting until the last minute actually served her.

13

TRUST AND CONTROL: WALKING THE LINE

One of the most difficult challenges parents face is navigating the delicate balance between freedom and control.

Parents are always walking the fine line between freedom and restrictions, connection and separation, trust and control. Learning how to walk this line allows us to both educate and protect our children, and is crucial to the fulfillment of our parental responsibilities. Becoming a masterful parent requires distinguishing where we do and do not have control over the decisions our children make. It means relinquishing our own need to control when the education or protection of our children does not require it. It means being fully aware of the possible consequences of trusting or controlling in each specific situation.

The father of a teenage boy told me that it drove him crazy when his son wore his pants "down around his knees". He firmly told his son that he was not to wear his paints in that manner. His son obeyed at home. What do you think happened when his son walked out the door?

A young woman confided how she, as well as most of her friends, coped with what she called "the parental fashion police". It was simple. In her locker she had two sets of clothing: one outfit for home and one for school.

The truth is, in most instances, we do not have control over our children's behavior. Our children know what we value and prefer, but each time our adolescent walks out the door they make their own decisions. This applies to smoking, drinking, sex, fashion as well as other areas of concern. Now this may seem to be a frightening admission of parental powerlessness, but in fact it is simply a realistic starting point for looking at where our parental influence begins and ends, and where the line is drawn between trust and control.

Usually worries arise from sensing that we have no control over our children in certain situations. We worry about our child when she goes to a party because we know, deep down, that we have no control over our 15-year-old once she walks out the door.

Our children are well aware of the values and behavior we support. From early on we have done the best we can to make our principles clear. A time comes when our children must make the choices they are going to make. Of course we hope that these choices reflect the values that we have taught them, but our children are going to do what they want to.

One of the most frustrating and frightening things kids do is choose friends who do not exemplify the behavior and values we profess. The truth is that often our children may unknowingly pick certain friends in order to learn very specific lessons. In these situations, their ability to stick to their values in the face of peer pressure is being tested. Often, when a morally challenging moment occurs, the voice of their parents wins out and they do the right thing.

176

Of course, we all know that there are also times when kids make decisions that do not serve them. This allows the possibility for learning by experience. How many of us took every word of warning or wisdom that was given to us when we were young and followed it to a "t"? For most of us, experience, rather than what we were told, has been our teacher. Our kids are entitled to this same route to maturity. They have to be free to make their own mistakes and learn from them. Think about it – we suffer and learn from our mistakes, as do our children. At the same time, experience can be a harsh teacher and we may legitimately wish to protect our children from situations that may be hurtful, overwhelming or could possibly defeat them. In other words, we have to choose when to exert control and when to allow our children to make their own decisions and discoveries. We have to walk the line between action and acceptance.

"KIDS TODAY SURE ARE DIFFERENT THAN WHEN I WAS YOUNG"

This is not just a cliche but in fact the truth. Educational psychologists have observed and measured characteristics and tendencies of today's youth that differ significantly from when we were their age. Because of these differences, approaches that were effective for our parents when we were youngsters may not be relevant for today's youth. Here are several of the qualities that they discovered about the current generation of young people:

- They come into the world with a feeling of royalty. They have the need for recognition and being acknowledged for their successes.

- They have the power to get attention in various ways - some of them negative.

- They believe in themselves and can be fearless.

- They have a problem with absolute authority (authority without explanation or choice).

- They often feel it's acceptable to do things differently. They may see a better way of doing things and can be labeled troublemakers.

- They are not shy about letting you know what they need.

- They are technologically oriented (e.g., computers and video games).

- They excel in an environment where boundaries are clearly set about what is and isn't acceptable but where open exploration within those boundaries is encouraged.

- They have excessive amounts of energy. They tend to bore easily, seem to have a low attention span and cannot sit still unless absorbed in something of their own interest.

- They usually test in at least one area of an IQ test in the "gifted" range.

- They have very high personal integrity and can see others' hidden agendas even when we can't.

- They are often very sensitive and as a result they need to feel safe and demand a great deal of attention.

- They have a deep compassion for other living things: plants, animals, the planet and other people.

- Eating is not such a big deal to them. They don't tend to consume large amounts of food.

- They value their freedom and feel most at home when they are given the opportunity to live spontaneously and instinctually.

- They value their privacy and personal space.

Even if your child does not fit these criteria, treating your child with compassion and respect is always preferable. Ask yourself: "Would I talk to my friends as disrespectfully as I sometimes speak to my children?"

HOW THEY NEED TO BE TREATED

Many of us were raised by angry, manipulative parents who, although doing the best they could, did not treat us (or each other) with integrity and respect. At some level, we bought into this way of being and accepted our parents' methods of control and discipline. Today, countless children are born with a level of self-respect that does not permit them to go along with a program based on manipulation, guilt, displaced anger and disrespect. Their integrity demands an explanation rather than being told, "do this because I say so." They do not respond well to orders but respect and listen to a loving and trusted confidante and counselor rather than a strict disciplinarian. They want people in their lives to demonstrate honesty, compassion and integrity not just in words but in their day-to-day interaction with them. This requires that when we become upset with some aspect of our child's behavior, we resist the impulse to react immediately and instead give ourselves a few minute "time out" to reflect on what is best for everyone concerned. **In other words our children require emotionally stable** and secure adults around them who respect and really listen to them.

As a result of their high awareness, sensitivity and honesty, they have little tolerance for inauthenticity and adults who demand rather than demonstrate respect. Kids today cannot be talked down to. Blind punishment doesn't usually work. It establishes fear and anger and invites more conflict. Instead, they need to be treated with respect along with being offered and held accountable for the consequences of the choices they make.

They may seem like a bundle of contradictions, but today's younger generation values freedom and thrives in an environment where their interests are respected. At the same time they crave the security that comes from being a "voting" member of the family. They know what they want and are strong-willed, yet also want to know that there are "boundaries" that cannot be crossed. They really don't want to be in charge but they do want to be honored. It is better to hear their reasons and consider their position carefully before responding to their desires rather than responding impulsively without thought. On the other hand, if you say no and then give in, they will quickly learn to pester you until they get what they want.

Many of today's children are more open, honest and in many ways wiser than we were at their age. Honor your child as a gift and a teacher rather than a burden. I know that this is extremely difficult at times but it comes under the heading of taking responsibility for the part your attitude has in affecting your relationship with your children.

HONORING YOUR CHILD'S UNIQUENESS

I often observe parents trying to control their children's energy rather than honoring its natural flow. I have heard a child complain of being hot and heard their parent respond, "No you're not. It's cold in here. Put on that sweater!"

The parents of a 14-year-old student battled every night with their daughter because she would not go to sleep at ten o'clock. But this girl was a straight A student!

The fact is that many of us work better at night. We need to respect our children's natural inclinations. Children are not all the same. Some children work more effectively while listening to music while others are thrown off by the slightest distraction. The performance of some children is enhanced by getting up and doing a different activity before returning to their homework. Others need to be encouraged to remain seated until their work is finished. Each of us has a different rhythm and flow. When it is honored, we experience joy and satisfaction.

Think about instances where your preoccupation with control interfered with allowing your child to grow and develop as a person. I remember the parents who did not permit their daughter to speak with boys after school or on the phone. I commented, "It is normal and healthy for a 14-year-old girl to want to interact with boys. In contrast most 10-year-old girls could care less about boys. It's a natural stage in an adolescent's growth. It's like telling a flower it's not the right time to bloom." They weren't impressed with my feedback. Two months later, upon arriving home from a trip a day earlier than expected, they found two boys with their shirts off jumping out of their bedroom window!

We need to listen and to respect the age appropriate requests of our children as opposed to imposing our need for control.

TO BE OR NOT TO BE

Our need to control also operates when we take a rigid position instead of considering more creative, flexible alternative approaches. We tend to play a certain character without being aware of it. Some parents continue to play the role of the cop even when they are not getting the desired results. This applies to any rigid role, even if it is the praiser, the conscious parent, the parent who is always calm or the parent who never worries. Even if our habitual role seems positive, it becomes counterproductive when it is not the best response in a given situation.

It is not appropriate to listen to your kids all the time. Sometimes it is appropriate to get angry. Just because your parents repressed your sexuality it may not be the best approach to always be liberal about sex. It may not be wise to always be the organizer, the cook or the negotiator. Playing only one character crushes our spontaneity. Being on automatic deprives our children of the opportunity to learn by experiencing these roles for themselves. For example, if we are always the cook, our children may never learn how to prepare their own food or experience the sense of accomplishment that comes from creating a delicious meal.

In order to feel connected to their parents, it is also important for children to feel that their parents and environments are "real". Quality time, which is very important, doesn't always have to be planned. The most rewarding times are often spent in unplanned, spontaneous and simple activities. Forced conversation at mealtimes does little to further connection and communication. On the other hand, casually going out to dinner with one child or simply coming into your child's room at bedtime provides a wonderful opportunity to connect. Believe it or not, sitting next to a child while communicating is often more effective than making eye-to-eye contact. **Taking time to explore and talk with your child about her interests can be one of the most effective ways to promote closeness.**

We have spoken about the importance of demonstrating the qualities of being a good listener, communicating assertively, forgiving, taking responsibility and accepting your child's reality. We can strive for these ideals but at times we are still at the mercy of reactive emotions. Sometimes we just "lose it" – we scream, say mean things or even slap our child. This behavior, although not to be praised, is part of being a "real" human being. After an emotional outburst, showing remorse and being concerned about your child's feelings can also be a significant way of connecting with your child. Being able to say you weren't proud of your actions and asking for forgiveness provides a wonderful lesson in the power of integrity and humility. It can restore our own self-esteem after an outburst that might otherwise leave us feeling ashamed of ourselves.

ANGER = LOSING CONTROL
BECAUSE YOU CAN'T CONTROL ALL THINGS

How many times have you been angry because you could not control a situation? For example, I once observed during class, the mother of a five-year-old repeatedly try to control her daughter's every movement. Whenever her daughter tried to explore her surroundings, she would grab her and say, "No". When her daughter touched something or asked if she could do something, her response was always the same, "No". Two weeks later when we were discussing communication skills, she said that it upset her that she was often angry with her daughter. I pointed out that her anger might be a reaction to her inability to control her daughter's every behavior rather than being pertinent to any of her daughter's particular behaviors.

Anger as a response to not being able to control reality occurs regularly: the light turns red, we're late, our friend is late, it's raining, our loved one doesn't call, the stock market tumbles, etc. In actuality we can be spoiled brats who get angry when we don't get our way.

It is also interesting to look at those instances when we don't outwardly express our anger but instead adopt another type of behavior as a reaction to not being in control, such as:

- Womanizing or misogyny as a manifestation of our anger at feeling controlled by a member of the opposite sex.

- Anorexia as an attempt to control one's life.

- Becoming a workaholic as an avoidance of the emotional upset caused by a broken relationship.

- Withholding sex or affection in a relationship as an expression of anger.

- Being a "nice person" and acting as if everything is okay, only to explode at another time or at another person.

The more we become aware of how much of our behavior is motivated by a need to control, the better able we are to choose more appropriate responses to life's challenges.

CONTROL, LIKE ANYTHING ELSE, IS A MATTER OF BALANCE

So far it might sound like I'm harping on the fact that control is bad and that parents should give up all control of their children. Nothing could be further from the truth. For the sake of balance, let's explore the other side of the control issue.

Children learn at a very early age how to play the control game. The two-year-old who wants a new toy cries hysterically in an attempt to wear us down. Our five-year-old cries and whines until we can't take it anymore and we give him what he wants. Our 16-year-old won't talk to us or intentionally gets lousy grades in order to "get even". This behavior is often motivated by a need for attention, trying to push our buttons or demonstrating independence by wanting it their own way. Regardless of the cause, children love to try to control parents. I have witnessed the sadness and frustration of parents who have lost control of their children.

Over time the parent–child connection is broken when the parent repeatedly loses control. When there are no more established boundaries, children inwardly lose a sense of safety and protection. **At a very deep level children equate discipline with caring.**

Regardless of age, it's critical for a child to sense that a parent is there for them. Even our seemingly tough adolescent needs to feel an envelope of safety in order to go out and explore and become independent. We convey this sense of caring through extending compassion, listening, instilling values, working hard at communication and enforcing discipline.

The goal of caring discipline is to teach children to control themselves. There is a profound difference between this approach and punishment motivated by forced control and revenge. Discipline inspired by teaching our children self control is exemplified by:

- Teaching consequences for actions rather than giving ultimatums.

- Being firm and staying calm rather than arguing.

- Allowing them to be bored at times, rather than feeling we have to constantly provide entertainment for them.

- Giving punishment that promotes learning rather than taking out our anger and frustration on them.

- Being consistent rather than reacting emotionally in the moment.

- Allowing them to be disappointed and frustrated when they don't get what they want rather than giving in.

- Giving positive feedback when they reinforce our values rather than harping on what a disappointment they are.

SAFE AT HOME

Our main function as parents is to assist in the formation of independent, functioning adults. In order for this to happen, children need to become aware of how they feel and what they want. When children are raised in a home where they feel it is safe to express their wants, needs and feelings, it is normal for them to challenge their parents from time to time. This is a natural, healthy and necessary part of children's development.

Do you value the development of your child's inner life, her sense of herself as a unique being? Are you exemplifying the truthfulness, flexibility, acceptance and honest communication that are necessary for this to happen? Or are peace and obedience at any price your goal? Does your child need to be a "good boy" or a "good girl" all the time in order to gain your approval? Did you have to behave a certain way and disown a part of yourself in order to be accepted by your parents?

I suggest you take some time to respond to these questions. This exploration could be quite revealing.

PARENTING STYLES RELATED TO CHILDREN'S SUCCESS

Research studies indicate that our children feel loved and cared for when parents set boundaries. But like anything else, it's all a matter of balance. If we are too rigid, they may stop trusting us, lie to us, become completely withdrawn or take their revenge by doing the opposite of our expectations. If we

184

are too permissive, we soon feel their exhaustion and irritability expressed in poor judgment and disrespect. There is a middle road that combines warmth, acceptance and involvement with firm behavioral control.

In his four year study, Lawrence Sternberg, a noted educational researcher, evaluated the effect that specific parenting styles had on the self-esteem, psychological well-being, substance abuse patterns and the academic performance of 20,000 adolescents from various cultural, ethnic and geographical areas. The qualities of acceptance, firmness and autonomy were used in distinguishing three styles of parenting: **authoritative**, **rigid** and **permissive**.

Authoritative parents view their main role as helping the child learn how to become self-reliant and personally responsible, as well as socially responsible and able to function as a member of a group. An authoritative parent promotes the child's freedom by valuing autonomy rather than control, by soliciting the child's opinions and by encouraging the child's full self-expression. Maturity is the goal rather than obedience or happiness. The child feels loved, valued and nurtured. These parents are coaches – dependable sources of guidance and assistance who are very aware of their children's emotional needs. As a result, their children have higher self-esteem, are better able to control their impulses, are more sociable, have a stronger sense of their own abilities and have a more enthusiastic outlook on life when compared to children raised by rigid or overly permissive parents. Adolescents raised by authoritative parents generally have higher grades, a more positive attitude toward schoolwork and are far less likely to abuse drugs and alcohol than those youths raised by permissive parents.

Rigid parents, on the other hand, are mainly concerned with controlling their child's impulses. Children raised by rigid parents have a psychological profile that suggests that they have been overpowered into obedience. They rate the same as children of authoritative parents regarding drug abuse and misbehavior. But these youngsters have lower self-esteem than other youngsters and are less self-reliant, less persistent and less socially poised. Their grades are almost as good as those raised by authoritative parents but they have a much lower view of their own competence and abilities and tend to live in fear of disapproval.

Permissive parents view their main responsibility as making sure the child is happy and the child's needs are gratified. Often, underlying this approach is the fear of being disliked by their children or just plain laziness. Children of permissive parents have higher drug and alcohol use than other adolescents. Their school performance is lower and their orientation toward school is weaker. They have a level of self-assurance, confidence and social poise comparable to that seen in the teenagers from authoritative households. But because their peers are of primary importance to them, they are more susceptible to their friends' influences. They are generally oriented more toward present pleasure and less towards future goals.

THE KEY INGREDIENTS

Masterful parenting requires that we recognize and make choices that serve ourselves and our families. In order to do this we must give up the rigidity caused by being stuck in habitual responses and belief patterns, and instead be alive to the possibilities of each moment. Sometimes it is appropriate to manipulate a situation. Other times it is essential to give up control and simply trust our children to make the right decision and act responsibly. When our options are wide open, as opposed to being limited by automatic ways of thinking and acting, our instincts and intuition come alive and we make choices that produce more fulfilling results. It's like having a whole toolbox full of tools, each one perfect for a unique situation, instead of trying to do everything with a hammer.

Amid all these choices and tools, the one thing that is constant and fundamental is the need to be loved. No matter who we are or what our age, we all seem to function better when we feel secure in our connection to someone we love. We all like to view ourselves as strong and independent, but the reality is that most of us function at a more fulfilled level when there is someone in our lives who we know is there for us. This is true for our children as well, even our adolescents. No matter how tough they may act, whether they let us see their needs or not, our children must know that we care – not the caring of sentiment or words alone but a caring demonstrated by how we listen and communicate and how we accept and forgive them. It's a caring demonstrated by treating our children in the way we have always wanted our parents to treat us.

TRUST AND CONTROL

1. LIST WHAT YOU WANTED MOST FROM YOUR PARENTS WHEN
    YOU WERE A CHILD.

188

2. NOW LIST WHAT YOU THINK YOUR CHILDREN WANT MOST
    FROM YOU.

CONTACT INFORMATION

Masterful Parenting was developed and refined over the past eleven years to serve as the course text for our eighteen-hour Parent Leadership Training. This training is offered by Education for Excellence Inc. (Dr. Marc Rosenbaum, director) which has presented courses to more than 4000 parents, teachers and students in New York City, California and Colombia. To find out more about our programs you can go to our website, www.ed4excellence.com.

To order copies of *Masterful Parenting* please call 800-591-5988, go to our website, ask your local bookstore to order a copy, or go to any of the major online bookstores. If you have any feedback regarding the book or are interested in bringing the Masterful Parenting programs to your area, please email marc@ed4excellence.com

189

190

CPSIA information can be obtained
at www.ICGtesting.com
Printed in the USA
FFOW02n0522010518
46410076-48196FF